P9-ELR-653

Ethiopia

Frontispiece: **Timket festival**

Consultant: Charles Schaefer, Professor of International Studies and History, Valparaiso University, Valparaiso, Indiana

Please note: All statistics are as up-to-date as possible at the time of publication.

Book production by The Design Lab

Library of Congress Cataloging-in-Publication Data
Names: Rogers Seavey, Lura. author.
Title: Ethiopia / By Lura Rogers Seavey.
Description: New York, NY : Children's Press, an imprint of Scholastic Inc., 2019. |
    Series: Enchantment of the world | Includes bibliographical references and index.
Identifiers: LCCN 2018016144 | ISBN 9780531130452 (library binding : alk. paper)
Subjects: LCSH: Ethiopia—Juvenile literature.
Classification: LCC DT373 .R64 2019 | DDC 963—dc23
LC record available at https://lccn.loc.gov/2018016144

Scholastic Inc., 557 Broadway, New York, NY 10012

1 2 3 4 5 6 7 8 9 10 R 28 27 26 25 24 23 22 21 20 19

Ethiopia

BY LURA ROGERS SEAVEY

Enchantment of the World™
Second Series

CHILDREN'S PRESS®

An Imprint of Scholastic Inc.

Contents

Left to right: **Erta Ale lava lake, ochre, calla lily, girls, gelada**

CHAPTER I

Welcome to Ethiopia

DRAMATIC MOUNTAINS, BROAD GRASSLANDS, THUN-
dering waterfalls. Ethiopia has all this and much
more. Over a hundred million people live in this
country in East Africa, making it the continent's second most
populated nation. People from dozens of different ethnic
groups live in Ethiopia's vibrant cities and varied landscapes.

Although the nation's capital, Addis Ababa, and other
cities are growing quickly, about 80 percent of Ethiopians still
live in the countryside. Some farm fertile soil, while others
move small herds of animals from waterhole to waterhole in
desert landscapes.

In Ethiopia, you can find the earth's longest-enduring lake
of bubbling lava, the world's rarest fox species, and one of
the hottest places on the planet, an area where people have
learned to live and work with hardly any water. The country

Opposite: **A group of
Ethiopian children. Nearly
half the population of
Ethiopia is under the age
of eighteen.**

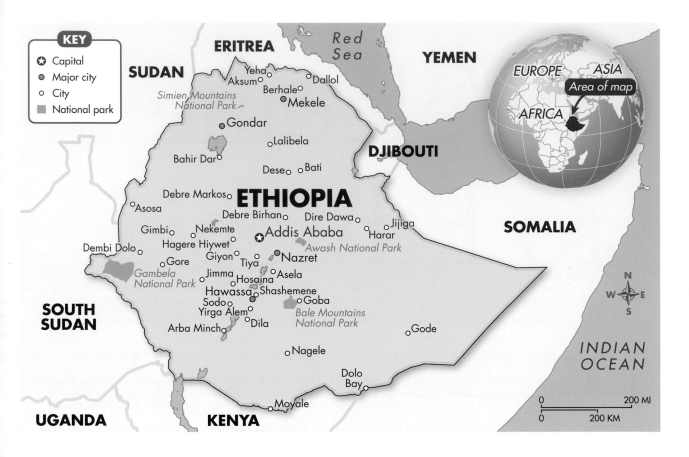

has active volcanoes and a scorching salt-crusted desert, but it also features fertile plateaus, lush tropical forests, and rushing rivers. It is the home of the world's best coffee, unique churches carved from solid rock, the oldest remains of our human ancestors, and a calendar that takes you back in time.

Ethiopia is the only nation in Africa that has never been colonized by foreigners—a fact Ethiopians are very proud of. Ethiopians are also proud of the fact that Christians and Muslims have lived together in their nation in relative peace for nearly 1,500 years, even as battles over religion have shaken other countries around the world. The Ethiopian Orthodox Church is the largest religious group in the country, but almost as many Ethiopians follow Islam.

The Ethiopian people have confronted many challenges over the years. They have faced drought and famine time and again. Yet they have proven themselves resilient. They continue to work hard to make a brighter future for themselves and their nation.

Members of the Karo ethnic group in southern Ethiopia are renowned for their use of body paint.

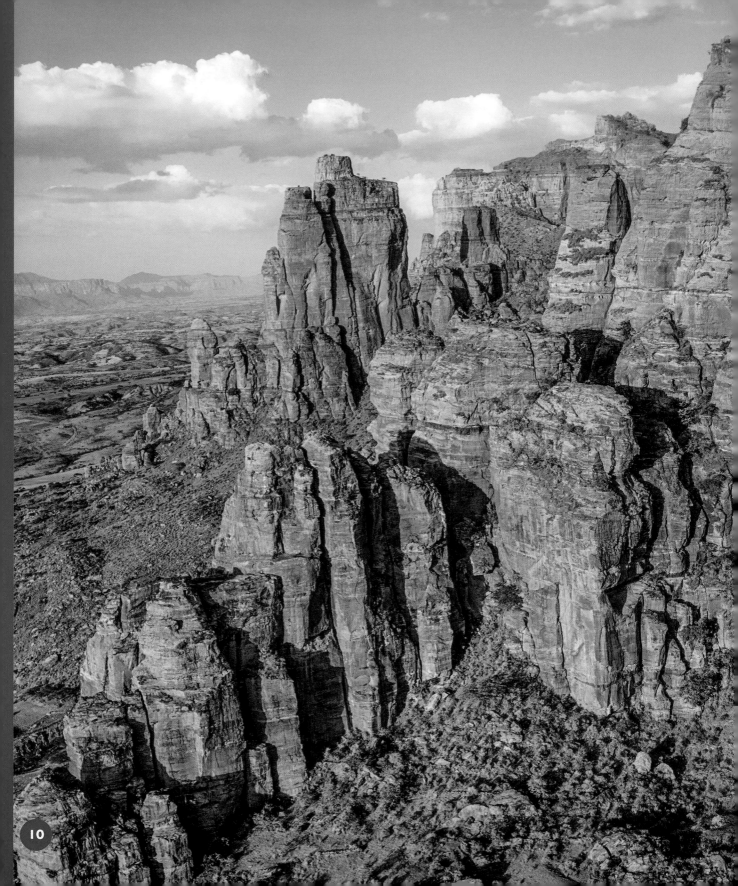

CHAPTER 2

A Varied Land

ETHIOPIA SITS IN EASTERN AFRICA, OCCUPYING MOST of what is called the Horn of Africa, a peninsula that juts out into the Indian Ocean. The Horn of Africa is named for its resemblance to a rhinoceros's horn.

Ethiopia is completely landlocked, separated from the Red and Arabian Seas to the east by the countries of Eritrea, Djibouti, and Somalia. To the south and west, it borders the countries of Kenya, South Sudan, and Sudan. It has an area of 426,373 square miles (1,104,300 square kilometers), which makes it nearly twice the size of the U.S. state of Texas.

The Great Rift Valley

Ethiopia is split in half by the Great Rift Valley, a section of the East African Rift System. This rift is a place where two tectonic plates—giant pieces of earth's outer layer that fit

Opposite: **The Gheralta Mountains of northern Ethiopia feature dramatic sandstone formations.**

Ethiopia's Extremes

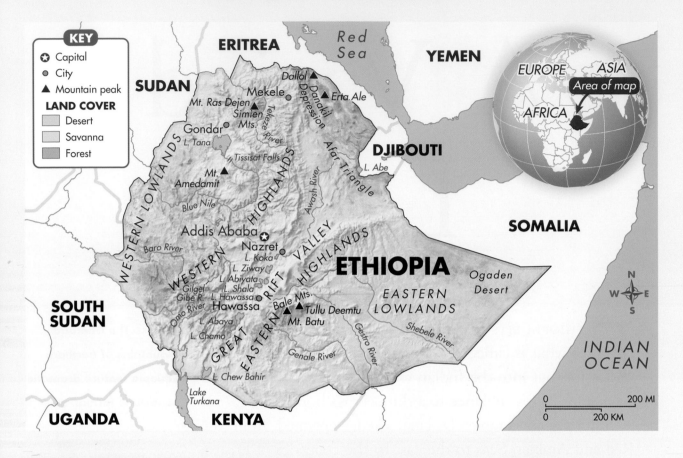

KEY
- ✪ Capital
- ○ City
- ▲ Mountain peak

LAND COVER
- Desert
- Savanna
- Forest

ERITREA — Red Sea — YEMEN
SUDAN
Dallol ▲
Mekele ○
Mt. Ras Dejen ▲
Simien Mts.
Gondar
L. Tana
Tekeze River
Danakil Depression
Erta Ale ▲
Afar Triangle
DJIBOUTI
L. Abe
Tissisat Falls
WESTERN HIGHLANDS
Mt. Amedamit ▲
Blue Nile
Addis Ababa ✪
Nazret
L. Koka
GREAT RIFT VALLEY
EASTERN HIGHLANDS
ETHIOPIA
Ogaden Desert
SOMALIA
Baro River
WESTERN LOWLANDS
L. Ziway
Gilgel Gibe R.
L. Abiyata
L. Shala
L. Hawassa
Hawassa
Bale Mts. ▲ ▲ Tullu Deemtu
Mt. Batu
EASTERN LOWLANDS
Shebele River
INDIAN OCEAN
SOUTH SUDAN
L. Abaya
Omo River
L. Chamo
EASTERN HIGHLANDS
GREAT RIFT VALLEY
Genale River
Gestro River
L. Chew Bahir
Lake Turkana
UGANDA
KENYA

EUROPE — ASIA
AFRICA
Area of map

N W E S

0 — 200 MI
0 — 200 KM

Highest Elevation: Ras Dejen, 14,872 feet (4,533 m) above sea level

Lowest Elevation: Kobar Sink in the Danakil Depression, 410 feet (125 m) below sea level

Highest Major City: Addis Ababa, 7,726 feet (2,355 m) above sea level

Largest Lake: Tana, 1,418 square miles (3,673 sq km) in the rainy season

Deepest Lake: Shala, 853 feet (260 m) deep

Largest Geographical Feature: Great Rift Valley, 1,700 miles (2,800 km) in Ethiopia, 3,700 miles (6,000 km) total in Africa

Hottest Place: Danakil Depression, with an average high temperature of 116°F (47°C) during summer months and 106°F (41°C) year-round

together like a puzzle—are pulling apart from one another. The result is that there is a long funnel-like shape running through Ethiopia, stretching from the Eritrean border in the northeast to the Kenyan border in the southwest. The East African Rift System is clearly visible from space.

Despite the fact that the rift forms a valley, more than half of it sits at an elevation higher than 4,000 feet (1,200 meters) above sea level. This is often referred to as the Upper Rift Valley, and occupies the central and southern portions of the Great Rift Valley. This is the most densely populated part of

The Great Rift Valley is about 50 miles (80 km) wide in Ethiopia.

the country because of its ideal farming conditions.

The northeastern section of the valley dips significantly lower, growing wider as it approaches the Red Sea. This region is home to many volcanoes, some active and some dormant. As a result of volcanic activity more than fifty million years ago, much of Ethiopia's land has deep layers of volcanic rock beneath the topsoil.

The Danakil Depression is the wide, low section of the Great Rift Valley that continues north into Eritrea. It is home to Ethiopia's lowest point, the Kobar Sink, which is 410 feet (125 m) below sea level.

The Bale Mountains in the Eastern Highlands feature a huge variety of landscapes, including fields of stone pinnacles created by the erosion of volcanic rock.

A lava lake on Erta Ale. To the local Afar people, Erta Ale is known as the "smoking mountain."

Living on the Fault Line

Volcanoes often form in cracks in the earth such as the Great Rift Valley. Ethiopia is home to a whopping fifty-nine volcanoes. Most have been dormant for thousands of years, but many remain active. Seven have erupted in the last one hundred years and three within the last fifteen years. One of these, Erta Ale, has an open lava lake. It has been present at least since the 1960s, making it the world's longest-existing lava lake, and one of only six worldwide.

Mountains and Lowlands

Nearly the entire length of the Great Rift Valley is bordered on both sides by mountains: the Western Highlands and the Eastern Highlands. The highlands then give way to the Western Lowlands and Eastern Lowlands.

The Western Highlands occupy a large portion of north and central Ethiopia. They are the most rugged region of

Colorful mineral deposits in the Danakil Depression

An Alien Landscape

The Danakil Depression is a desert region containing some of the most extreme conditions in the world. It is part of the Afar Triangle, where three tectonic plates meet. These plates are slowly moving apart, by about 0.5 to 1 inch (1 to 2.5 centimeters) per year. The Danakil Depression is home to the Dallol volcano and its hydrothermal fields. The hydrothermal fields contain hot springs and geysers that bring salt, sulfur, potash, and other minerals to the surface, where they evaporate, leaving colorful deposits. Where the minerals have not evaporated, small lakes boil, thick with chemicals.

The only life that can survive in these extreme conditions are microbes called extremophiles. Because these unusual organisms can live in such extreme conditions, scientists study them to try to figure out how life might be able to exist on other planets.

The Afar people, who live in the Danakil Depression, have adapted to the hot and arid land. They depend on water from the Awash, a river that dries up long before it reaches the sea. They also harvest the salt deposits to sell.

Ethiopia. The highest peak in the Western Highlands—and in the entire country—is Mount Ras Dejen (or Dashen), which reaches 14,872 feet (4,533 m) above sea level. The Western Lowlands occupy the western border along Sudan and South Sudan. The soil here is dense and clay-based, which can make farming difficult.

The Eastern Highlands are smaller than the Western Highlands. The twin peaks of Tullu Deemtu and Mount Batu are the highest in this range, both topping 14,000 feet (4,300 m). The Eastern Lowlands drop off to the southeast, with the lowest elevations along the southern border with Somalia. The easternmost section of this is the Ogaden region, home to the Ogaden Desert. Oil and gas deposits are scattered throughout the desert, but most of these resources remain untapped. Crops are successful here if they are watered by irrigation, but farming is not sustainable if it depends on natural rainfall.

Camels for sale at a livestock market in the Ogaden region. Camels are commonly used to transport goods through this desert area.

People walk through historic arches near the royal palace in Gondar.

Urban Landscapes

Ethiopia's largest city is its capital, Addis Ababa, which is home to about 3,273,000 people. The nation's other cities are much smaller. Ethiopia's second-largest city is Nazret, also called Adama, which has a population of about 324,000. Nazret is an important center of industry with many factories and processing plants. It sits southeast of Addis Ababa on a rail line and is active in the import and export trade. It is also a popular tourist destination because it is close to Lake Ziway and Awash National Park.

Gondar, the nation's third-largest city with a population of 323,900, has a rich history. From 1632 to 1855, it was the capital of the Ethiopian Empire. Because of its prominence, many castles and historic churches were built there. Today, it is a busy, modern city known for its community of craftspeople who work with cloth, metal, and leather. It is also the center of Ethiopia's small Jewish community.

Mekele, home to 323,700 people, is located on the western edge of the Danakil Depression. Mekele has been a center of the salt trade for centuries and has become an important food processing and trade city. It is an increasingly popular tourist destination.

Tall office buildings rise behind a mosque in Mekele.

Rivers and Lakes

Ethiopia contains several different river systems. The largest and most significant begins in the Western Highlands. Mountain runoff feeds into the Blue Nile, the Tekeze, and the Baro Rivers. These three rivers meander westward, eventually feeding into the White Nile in Sudan and South Sudan. The Blue Nile is the primary source of the great Nile River that flows through Egypt. Although the Blue Nile flows from Lake Tana, the largest lake in Ethiopia, its actual source is a small mountain spring southwest of the lake near Mount Amedamit. This spring is

In northern Ethiopia, a hydroelectric dam was built on the Tekeze River, creating Tekeze Lake.

considered holy, with healing waters that Christian Orthodox pilgrims travel hundreds of miles to reach.

Not far from Lake Tana, the river spectacularly flows over Tissisat Falls, also called the Blue Nile Falls. This is an impressive sight, as the river plunges 138 feet (42 m) and creates a spray that can travel up to a half mile (1 km) during the wettest season. During the rainy season, the falls spread, reaching over 1,300 feet (400 m) wide. The region surrounding the falls is lush, green, and full of wildlife.

The Blue Nile flows for approximately 500 miles (800 km) within Ethiopia's borders, and another 400 miles (600 km) before reaching the White Nile. Exact measurements are difficult to

Tissisat Falls means "smoking water" in the Amharic language. The falls got their name from the clouds of mist the Blue Nile creates as it crashes over the ledge.

A fisher rows a traditional boat made of reeds in Lake Tana.

Lake Tana

Lake Tana is Ethiopia's largest lake, stretching as much as 41 miles (66 km) wide and 52 miles (84 km) long during the rainy season. It is a relatively shallow lake with the deepest place being only 49 feet (15 m) deep.

Many kinds of wildlife live in the lake, including twenty-eight species of fish that are caught for sale. It is common to see fishers in traditional papyrus reed boats, called *tanquas*, pulling up along the shore to sell their catch directly from the boats. In addition to fish, the lake is home to many other animals, including hippopotamuses and Nile monitors, the largest lizards in Africa.

The lake's thirty-seven islands are covered in dense forests that harbor wildlife such as beautiful colobus monkeys, hyenas, and small antelopes called duikers. On several of the islands are old monasteries featuring fantastic murals and relics.

determine because the course runs in part through extremely deep mountain gorges where it is impossible to travel. The Blue Nile is an important source of water for irrigation and hydroelectric power, with five dams harnessing its energy.

In the Upper Rift Valley, eight major lakes formed as water drained down from the surrounding highlands. These lakes, Koka, Ziway, Langano, Abiyata, Shala, Awasa, Abaya, and

A boy leaps down the
bank of the Omo River,
the largest river in
southern Ethiopia.

Chamo, sit at elevations of 4,000 feet (1,200 m) and 5,600
feet (1,700 m) above sea level. The largest of these is Abaya.
Langano is the only lake that is safe to swim in because a
chemical in it prevents bilharzia, a blood disease. The Omo
River drains to the southwest from the Upper Rift Valley,
eventually emptying into Lake Turkana, which spans the border into Kenya. The Awash flows from the northern section
of the upper valley, northeast to Lake Abe, which Ethiopia
shares with Djibouti.

Streams in the Eastern Highlands feed into the Genale
and Shebele Rivers, and the smaller Gestro River. All of these
flow southeast into Somalia, where they eventually join and
empty into the Indian Ocean. There are no major rivers that
extend through the eastern Ogaden region.

Climate

Ethiopia lies in the tropical latitudes, the part of the earth
that surrounds the equator and generally has a warm climate.
In Ethiopia, the climate varies a great deal depending on

elevation. In general, higher elevations have more temperate conditions while lower areas are hotter and drier.

The year in Ethiopia can be divided into seasons based on rainfall. The *kremt* is Ethiopia's long rainy season, also known as the "big rains." It generally lasts from June through August. September through February brings a long dry season, with November and December seeing the lowest temperatures. From March through April is the *belg*, or "small rains." This is also a period of hot temperatures, with May being the hottest.

The highlands and parts of the Upper Rift Valley enjoy a temperate climate. Temperatures sometimes drop as low as

Clouds frequently sit among the peaks of the Simien Mountains.

32 degrees Fahrenheit (0 degrees Celsius) during November, December, and January at altitudes over 8,200 feet (2,500 m). The capital city of Addis Ababa, which sits in the highlands, reaches an average high of 78°F (25°C) in March, the city's hottest month. The rainiest region is the southern part of the Western Highlands, where as much as 80 inches (200 cm) can fall each year. The northern section of both the Western and Eastern Highlands gets an average of 55 inches (140 cm) of rain annually.

The lowlands have a drier, warmer climate. As the elevation decreases, the land becomes either the grassy plains of a savanna or the desert, depending on the amount of rainfall and the water supply from rivers. The Eastern Lowlands

Girls run through the rain in Addis Ababa, where the summer months are the wettest.

A plateau in northern Ethiopia has been deeply eroded, forming the Simien Mountains, now the site of a national park.

Protecting Nature

To protect the dwindling habitats of the plants and animals that live in Ethiopia, the government has established twenty national parks, along with several wildlife sanctuaries and reserves. One of the oldest, Awash National Park, opened in 1966. It covers woodlands and grasslands and has beautiful waterfalls along the Awash River.

The country's best known national parks are Simien Mountains National Park and Bale Mountains National Park. These two highland parks are renowned because they have some of the rarest and most remarkable species, including the Simien fox, the giant mole-rat, and an antelope called the mountain nyala.

The nation's largest national park is Gambela National Park, which protects swamps and wetlands near the South Sudanese border. Wildlife abounds in Gambela. There are elephants, giraffes, cheetahs, and vast herds of white-eared kobs and other antelopes.

have shortened rainy seasons during April/May and October/November, with the least amount of rain falling in the Ogaden Desert. The Eastern Lowlands are hotter, home to the Danakil Desert, which can reach over 122°F (50°C). This region receives little to no rain.

CHAPTER 3

Wild Things

ETHIOPIA'S PLANTS AND ANIMALS ARE AS VARIED AS its landscape. The nation is home to lush forests with abundant wildlife as well as deserts where only a few plants and animals have adapted to survive. Both soil conditions and rainfall influence which plants and animals live in which areas. The wetter and more temperate parts of the highlands have the greatest vegetation, while lower elevations tend to have smaller forests and more areas with low grass. Hotter, drier regions are dotted with desert shrubs, with small green areas surrounding the occasional water sources. Only a few animal species live there.

Opposite: **The gelada is sometimes called the bleeding heart monkey because of the red heart-shaped patch in the center of its chest.**

Plant Life

Many different kinds of trees grow in the highlands, including junipers, pines, and figs. The Ethiopian rose, the only rose

Symbol of Peace

The calla lily, sometimes called the Arum lily, is often considered the national flower of Ethiopia. It grows to a height of 2 to 3 feet (0.6 to 1 m) and has a pointed funnel-like flower that is usually white. The calla lily grows best in soil that remains moist. It is abundant in Ethiopia, where it is a symbol of peace and is also valued for its lovely fragrance and graceful shape.

All parts of the calla lily are poisonous to humans and animals.

native to Africa, is also found in the highlands. It has berries full of vitamins that have helped Ethiopians during famine. The Bale Mountains are home to many different kinds of flowers, including the red-hot poker, which has spiky orange flowers that attract hummingbirds.

The durable teff plant is a native crop that has been grown by Ethiopians since 4000 BCE. It grows in the highlands and can withstand both wet and drought conditions. It also grows quickly and provides many different nutrients, making it a very important food source for both people and livestock. A bread called injera is made from teff and is a common part of Ethiopian cuisine. Teff has also become popular in Europe and North America as a health food because of its high fiber content and because, unlike wheat, it is gluten free.

The highlands are also home to Ethiopia's most valuable

crop, coffee. It is native to the region, and Ethiopians are credited with being the first to grow coffee for the beverage made from its beans.

Ensete is a staple crop primarily grown by the Gurage people of southwestern Ethiopia. Although the plant is related to the banana, it is the root rather than the fruit that people eat. The root and the inner bark are ground to make a paste that is used in breads. Ensete has been valuable during times of famine because it can survive drought, and each plant produces

The wild fig trees of Ethiopia have massive trunks. The trees produce fruit that are an important source of food.

The fruit on a coffee plant turns red as it ripens. The beans used to make coffee are the seeds of the fruit.

Kaffa's Gift

The coffee plant is native to the Ethiopian highlands. Although the plant is a source of income for many Ethiopians, it is also valued for other reasons. Ethiopia was the first place in the world where the coffee plant was treasured for its fruit and the first place where the popular beverage was brewed. The name of the plant comes from the Kaffa region where it was first cultivated.

There are many legends about the discovery of coffee as we know it, but the most widely told story takes place around 900 CE and concerns a goat herder named Kaldi. One day Kaldi noticed that his goats were unusually energetic after munching the berries from a plant, and tried a few of the berries himself. After finding that he too had more energy, his wife suggested that he bring the berries to a nearby monastery because they must be a gift from God. The first monk

he spoke to threw them in the fire, convinced that they were the work of the devil. The fire began to roast the beans, and the other monks came to find out what the wonderful smell was. After crushing the beans to put out the burning embers, the monks placed the remains in water and discovered that a tasty beverage resulted.

Historians agree that Ethiopian monks were the first to cultivate and roast coffee for drinking. By 1615, coffee was being exported to Europe. Nearly half of the coffee produced in Ethiopia is consumed there. The rest is a valuable export.

The coffee plant thrives in moderate climates at an altitude of around 5,000 feet (1,500 m). Because of climate change, however, growers are gradually being forced to move coffee plantations to higher ground as temperatures rise.

roughly 90 pounds (40 kilograms) of edible parts when it is harvested. The nonedible parts of the thick, sturdy plant are used for construction and making tools.

The eucalyptus tree grows in the highlands, although it is not native to Ethiopia. It was brought from Australia to combat deforestation, especially around the capital city of Addis Ababa. It was chosen because it grows quickly, so it can provide firewood and building material. Eucalyptus, however, needs more water to grow than Ethiopia's native plants and trees. Today, Ethiopians are making an effort to again grow native tree species that replenish the nutrients in soil rather than depleting them.

The ensete plant is used to make the roofs on the traditional homes of the Dorze people of southern Ethiopia. These tall plants can be seen growing behind the houses.

Bird Life

Ethiopia is home to more than eight hundred species of birds, making it a popular destination for bird-watchers. All kinds of birds pass through the region, including eagles, goshawks, pigeons, doves, falcons, and warblers. Waterbirds that live in Ethiopia include storks, ducks, geese, and cranes. Many varieties of vultures and buzzards live in Ethiopia, eating the carcasses of dead animals. Bearded vultures sometimes grab small live animals, including young gelada monkeys.

A man feeds fish to a group of great white pelicans in Lake Awasa. These birds need to eat 2 to 3 pounds (1 to 1.5 kg) of fish per day.

Many bird species are endemic to Ethiopia, meaning they are found nowhere else in the world. The blue-winged goose lives in areas more than 6,000 feet (1,800 m) above sea level, preferring marshy wetlands. The banded barbet, meanwhile, lives in fig trees in the highlands. The wattled ibis is found only in Ethiopia and neighboring Eritrea. It prefers to nest in the cliffs at elevations above 5,000 feet (1,500 m), usually overlooking rivers and lakes. More colorful birds endemic to Ethiopia and Eritrea include the green parrot called the black-winged lovebird, and the bright yellow Abyssinian oriole.

The Abyssinian oriole often lives in woodlands, where it feeds on insects, berries, and other fruit.

Mammals

Ethiopia's woodlands and savannas support many kinds of mammals. Wild dogs, hyenas, foxes, and jackals are found in abundance throughout Ethiopia, in all climates except the most extreme desert. A large variety of species live in the lowlands, especially in the savanna and near bodies of water. Rugged wild pigs called warthogs feed on grass, eggs, insects, and whatever else they can find. Antelopes such as waterbucks, gazelles, and oryx graze on the grasses and leaves. More than a dozen species of monkeys also live in Ethiopia, including the black-and-white colobus, the vervet monkey, and the gelada.

Giraffes live in southeastern Ethiopia. The legs of these towering animals are longer than the height of many adult men.

The Abyssinian lion is notable for its dark mane.

Symbol of Strength

Ethiopia's national animal is the Abyssinian lion, which is also called the Addis Ababa lion. The lion has been a symbol of bravery and strength for Ethiopia over the years as the country fought to maintain its independence. Because of hunting and loss of habitat, the Abyssinian lion is now endangered. Only about 1,700 remain, mostly in the savannas.

Giraffes amble across the lowlands and the Rift Valley. Small populations of elephants, rhinoceroses, and lions also live in these regions. Elephants live in the plateaus, and hippopotamuses enjoy the water at Lake Tana and other year-round bodies of water.

Many rodents live in Ethiopia, including dozens of species of mice, rats, gerbils, squirrels, and shrews. Other smaller mammals found in Ethiopia include hares, hedgehogs, and cat species such as the Abyssinian wildcat.

Geladas spend hours each day grazing. Using both hands, they pluck as many as 150 blades of grass a minute.

The Grass-Eating Monkey

The gelada, a long-haired monkey found only in the mountainous regions of Ethiopia, is sometimes called the lion baboon because of the fluffy mane-like fur that grows all around its face. It is, in fact, not a baboon at all.

Most geladas live in the high grasslands of the Simien Mountains. They spend almost all their time on the ground. Their primary food is grass. Although many species of grass-eating monkeys once existed, all except for geladas have become extinct.

Geladas have short fingers, but an amazingly strong grip that allows them to climb safely and to move quickly across rocky terrain.

This is especially important since they sleep perched on cliffs to stay safe from nighttime predators like hyenas and leopards. They also have fang-like teeth that they can use to defend themselves if attacked.

These monkeys are very social, living in large groups of sometimes 1,200 animals. They make an unusually wide variety of sounds to communicate, including barks, grunts, shrieks, and squeals.

Now, about two hundred thousand geladas live in Ethiopia. Their numbers are decreasing, however, as agriculture expands in the region where they live, infringing on their habitat.

Endangered Creatures

The rarest animals in Ethiopia are found in the mountain regions, especially in the Simien and Bale Mountains. It is here that the last of the Simien foxes are found. They hunt smaller mammals, of which their favorite prey is the giant mole-rat. This large rodent lives in burrows, which it digs with large fang-like teeth that it also uses for defense. Because of a dwindling habitat, giant mole-rats are now endangered.

The walia ibex is a critically endangered species that lives only in the Simien Mountains. This wild goat lives on the

Both male and female walia ibex have horns. The males' horns are larger, however, sometimes reaching 6 feet (2 m) in length.

ledges and rocky cliffs. Although it is preyed on by few species, the main reason for its rarity is that humans have often hunted it. Today, there are only around five hundred left. The mountain nyala, which is unique to the Bale Mountains, has a population of only around four thousand. This antelope was not officially discovered until 1908.

Only a few hundred tall, elegant Simien foxes survive.

In Danger

The Simien fox, which is found only in Ethiopia, is Africa's most endangered carnivore. Currently only about five hundred of these striking creatures remain, most living in the Bale Mountains. They are the height of a large dog, and their fur is rust colored with white on the belly and throat. They have exceptionally fluffy tails and tall, pointed ears.

The fox lives in the highlands, generally at elevations higher than 10,000 feet (3,000 m). Their main source of food is the giant mole-rat. They live in family groups that join to form larger packs.

Their biggest threat is humans turning their habitat into farmland. The foxes are also threatened by disease.

A researcher takes a hair sample of a sedated Simien fox.

CHAPTER 4

Then and Now

Human life has a long history in Ethiopia. Some fossilized bones that have been discovered in Ethiopia are more than three million years old. They belonged to species that are the ancestors of modern humans.

Modern humans, *Homo sapiens*, evolved in Africa more than 300,000 years ago and eventually spread around the world. *Homo sapiens* fossils that are 160,000 years old have been discovered in the Awash Valley of Ethiopia. By about three thousand years ago, people in what is now Ethiopia were using plows to grow crops. Soon thereafter, kingdoms arose.

Early Kingdoms

The mythology about the origins of Ethiopian civilization, recorded in a collection of stories called the *Kebra Negast*, claims that the first known dynasty of Ethiopia, the Solomonid

Famous Fossils

On November 24, 1974, in the Awash Valley of central Ethiopia, archaeologists uncovered the bones of an early hominid, a human ancestor 3.5 million years old. From the fragments found, the archaeologists were able to determine that this hominid was a young adult female about 3.5 feet (1 m) tall who weighed about 65 pounds (30 kg) when she died. From the shape and the size of the bones, scientists determined that she walked upright on two feet, rather than on four feet as apes typically do.

The archaeologists named her Lucy after the popular Beatles song "Lucy in the Sky with Diamonds," which was played frequently in the camp where the fossils were being unearthed. Ethiopians call her Dinkenesh, which means "wonderful" in Amharic, the most common language spoken in the region.

Lucy's fossils are renowned worldwide because of their contribution to the study of human evolution. The fragile remains are stored in a special safe in the National Museum of Ethiopia in Addis Ababa. Replicas of the bones are on display in the gallery.

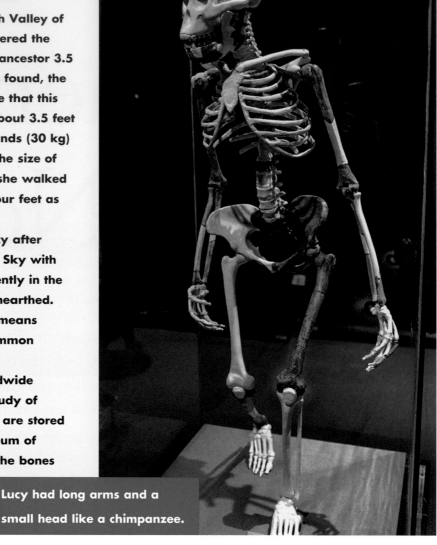

Lucy had long arms and a small head like a chimpanzee.

dynasty, began with emperor Menelik I. According to legend, Menelik was the son of the Queen of Sheba, a ruler in Arabia, and King Solomon of Jerusalem. This dynasty lasted from around 1000 BCE to the seventh century BCE, when the Kingdom of Da'amat was established.

The Da'amat capital city was built in Yeha, in what is now northern Ethiopia. It was an impressive agricultural center, where farmers irrigated crops and used ox-drawn plows. The city was also known for its weapons and tools made of iron, and for its booming trade.

When trade routes began to shift away from the Da'amat capital, the inland Kingdom of Aksum began to rise to power. It was centered in what are now southern Eritrea and northern Ethiopia, and spread south and west. The kingdom flourished from the first century CE to the early eighth century. It became the Red Sea's major trade center between Africa and Asia.

During the fourth century CE in the Kingdom of Aksum, towering obelisks were carved to serve as grave markers.

Christianity was introduced to the region during the fourth century, and the Ethiopian Orthodox Church quickly took hold. Muslims also arrived in the region during the Aksumite era, in the seventh century. Political changes in southern Arabia in the early eighth century eventually led to the end of trade with Aksum, and the kingdom began to decline.

The Zagwe Dynasty

After the decline of the Aksumites, the seat of power moved south. By the late twelfth century, the Agau people had established the Zagwe dynasty. The city of Roha, which is now Lalibela, was their capital. The Zagwe family claimed to be descended from King Solomon, giving them a divine right to rule as descendants of Menelik I. King Lalibela, who reigned from 1185 to 1225, is the most famous of the Zagwe emperors. He is best remembered for supporting Christianity and working to create a unified culture in the countryside. In 1270, a prince named Yekuno Amlak from Amhara led a revolt against the Zagwe royalty. He was helped by several church leaders who claimed that his family was descended from King Solomon, making him the true heir to the kingdom. Thus, a new bloodline took power.

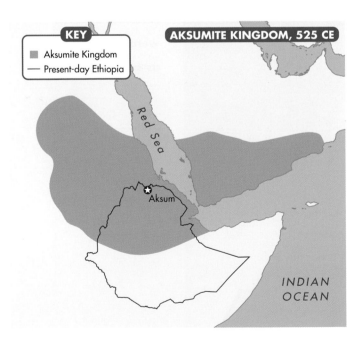

KEY

Aksumite Kingdom
Present-day Ethiopia

AKSUMITE KINGDOM, 525 CE

Red Sea

Aksum

INDIAN OCEAN

A man pulls himself up a thick rope to reach the church of Debre Damo.

Debre Damo: A Mountaintop Church

At the summit of an *amba*, a flat-topped mountain in northern Ethiopia, is a monastery that was built in the sixth century CE. The oldest church building in Ethiopia that remains in its original form, Debre Damo is still an active monastery and can be visited only by men. To get there, visitors must climb a 78-foot (24 m) length of rope up the side of a sheer cliff.

According to legend, the monastery was founded when Abba Aregawi, an early monk in the Ethiopian Orthodox Church, discovered the plateau and thought it would be a good place to live as a hermit. God then ordered a snake to stretch down from the cliff and lift the holy man to the top.

To construct the monastery, monks built a wooden ramp to the cliff top so they could carry up supplies. After the monastery was completed, they destroyed the ramp. Since that time, the rope has been the only way to get to the monastery. The church, which is decorated with paintings and with wood carvings of animals, houses precious decorated manuscripts, one of which is the oldest in Ethiopia.

This was a very active time for the Ethiopian Orthodox Church, when they built many of their biggest and most impressive churches and monasteries. While Christianity was growing in the more populated central regions of what is now Ethiopia, Islam was gaining followers in the periphery to the east and south.

Invasions and Unrest

In about 1530, a Muslim leader named Amam Ahmed (popularly referred to as Ahmed Gragn, "the left-handed") set out on a holy war, or jihad, against the Christian peoples of Ethiopia. Portugal was active in trade during this period, and the conflict made it more difficult for the Portuguese to conduct trade using the Red Sea. Because of this, in 1541 Portugal sent troops to train the Ethiopian Christians to fight against the jihad. In 1543, the Ethiopians and Portuguese defeated Ahmed Gragn, ending the war.

The Portuguese decided to stay in Ethiopia. They began to try to convert the Ethiopians to the Roman Catholic Church. Eventually, both Christians and Muslim Ethiopians became determined to end this foreign interference. They worked together to drive the Portuguese out.

The Age of Princes

During the unrest, Oromo people from the south began to spread north and take over parts of the existing empire. The capital city was moved farther north to Gondar. Eventually the Oromo kingdoms became part of the larger empire, helped along by a marriage between royal families. By 1700, Gondar had become an important city for education, the arts, and trade.

This period, known as the Zemene Mesafint, or the Age of Princes, was an era of progress for the wealthy classes. The name also referred to the fact that there was not a strong central ruler. Instead, several Ethiopian princes controlled regions and extracted their wealth and power by exploiting

the peasants around them. Under this feudal system, it was common for farmers to pay high taxes on their crops and for people to be forced to serve the local royalty.

The British expedition to rescue missionaries and explorers included thirteen thousand soldiers and forty thousand animals, including forty-four elephants.

The Beginnings of Modern Ethiopia

The crowning of Emperor Tewodros II in 1855 was the beginning of a new unified Ethiopia that would become the country that exists today. Tewodros tried to abolish the feudal system and increase loyalty to the government. He also wanted to modernize the army. He tried to convince the British to join him in a war against Islam, but they ignored his request. He responded by having British missionaries and explorers captured and thrown in jail. To retaliate against the Ethiopians and rescue those who had been captured, in 1868 the British sent in troops to attack Tewodros's forces. Tewodros killed himself to avoid capture after his troops were defeated.

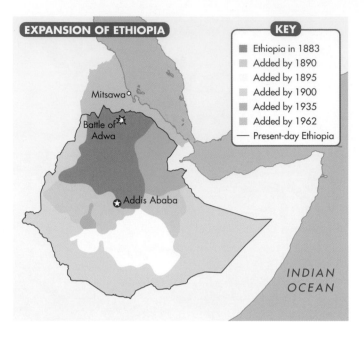

EXPANSION OF ETHIOPIA

KEY

- Ethiopia in 1883
- Added by 1890
- Added by 1895
- Added by 1900
- Added by 1935
- Added by 1962
- — Present-day Ethiopia

Mitsawa

Battle of Adwa

Addis Ababa

INDIAN OCEAN

After a few years of conflict, Emperor Yohannes IV was crowned in 1872. During his rule, he expanded the empire to the south and east, reclaiming part of the coast, what is now Eritrea, from the Egyptians.

Soon after that victory, however, Italian troops landed at Mitsawa (the present-day city of Massawa) and began their attempt to colonize Ethiopia. The Italians were prevented from moving inland, though a few thousand troops remained along the coast. Yohannes ruled through 1889, when he was killed in battle while fighting an invading army from neighboring Sudan.

The Reign of Menelik II

Emperor Menelik II took the throne almost immediately. He took a different approach to the Italian threat. Instead of fighting, he signed the Treaty of Wichale, which gave Italy control over Eritrea. He signed two copies, one in Amharic and one in Italian. He soon found out that the Italian version granted Italy diplomatic and economic control over Ethiopia, so he began to gather military equipment in order to protect his nation. After five years of building up weapons and food for his army, one hundred thousand Ethiopian troops defeated a smaller Italian army at the Battle of Adwa in March 1896.

An Ethiopian Triumph

In 1896, Ethiopian troops triumphed in a battle against Italian forces who were attempting to colonize their nation. The Battle of Adwa remains Ethiopia's iconic historical event. At the time, the rest of Africa was being carved up among European colonial powers. But Ethiopia, a black nation, had defeated a white, European state. Ethiopia became the beacon of all African nations and peoples. The battle also humiliated the Italians. Today, the Victory of Adwa is a public holiday across Ethiopia.

Menelik II at the Battle of Adwa

By the end of 1896, Ethiopia and Italy had signed a new treaty that guaranteed Ethiopian independence.

During the remainder of his rule, Menelik II expanded Ethiopian territory to the south until it reached its current borders. He also focused on building his new capital city, Addis Ababa, in the center of the country and ordered the construction of a railway from Addis Ababa to the port at Djibouti.

After Menelik II died in 1913, his grandson Iyasu took the throne. Iyasu's father was originally Muslim but had converted to Christianity. Iyasu spent his time as emperor trying to reduce religious and ethnic tensions in the country. Ethiopia's leadership had traditionally been Christian, but he began appointing more Muslims to important positions. This angered many members of the Christian ruling class. Iyasu was removed from power in 1916.

The Rule of Haile Selassie

Iyasu was replaced by Menelik's daughter Zauditu, who was not allowed to rule on her own. Her father's cousin Ras Tafari Makonnen was appointed regent and placed in charge of the empire. As regent, Ras Tafari brought Ethiopia into an international organization called the League of Nations, which had been established after World War I in an effort to maintain peace. The country's economy grew during these years, with the growth of the coffee industry and trade.

After Zauditu's death in 1930, Ras Tafari became emperor and was crowned Haile Selassie I. In leading the country, he focused on trade with other nations and on building a more modern government, including the creation of a parliament.

His progress got the attention of Italian fascist leader Benito Mussolini, who wanted to have complete control over eastern Africa and avenge Italy's humiliation in the Battle of Adwa. In October 1935, Italian forces attacked Ethiopia. They quickly defeated Haile Selassie's army, and Haile Selassie went into exile.

The Last Emperor

Ethiopia's last emperor was given the name Ras Tafari (Ras means "king") as a child. He was born near the city of Harar, to Ras Makonnen, a relative and adviser to Emperor Menelik II. He ruled the empire for fourteen years as regent to Empress Zauditu, and officially became emperor after her death in 1930. As emperor, he was known as Haile Selassie.

Haile Selassie worked to modernize Ethiopia. His policies were considered progressive, and he is known for creating the first paid civil service positions in the government. He also wanted the countries to work together. He was important in the creation of the Organization of African Unity (now the African Union), an international group devoted to cooperation among African nations.

After ruling Ethiopia for much of the twentieth century, Haile Selassie was forced from power in 1974.

Haile Selassie was thirty-eight years old when he was crowned emperor in 1930.

Between 1936 and 1941, Italy occupied Ethiopia while Ethiopian patriots continued to resist. Italy combined Ethiopia with Eritrea and a region then called Italian Somaliland to form Italian East Africa. When World War II broke out in 1939, allied countries such as Great Britain and France led the fight against the Axis powers, Germany, Italy, and Japan. With the help of British forces, Haile Selassie returned to power in 1941.

After the war, the United Nations ruled that Eritrea should be part of Ethiopia. In 1952, the two countries joined, and Ethiopia once again gained the strategic port at Mitsawa.

In the 1950s, Ethiopia continued to modernize. The education and communications systems grew, and coffee exporting

Haile Selassie (left) greets a Rastafarian leader in Jamaica in 1966. The Rastafarian religion takes its name from Haile Selassie's original name, Ras Tafari, and many Rastafarians believe that Haile Selassie was the messiah of the black people.

thrived. Meanwhile, many Eritreans were opposed to Ethiopia and Eritrea being joined together. By the early 1960s, an independence movement was active in Eritrea. This movement would cause upheaval in Ethiopia for years to come.

Communists Take Control

Despite Haile Selassie's attempts to modernize the government, he remained dedicated to keeping many parts of the monarchy, and revolutionary sentiment began to build. Many people believed that the monarchy was holding the country back. By the 1970s, student-led communist parties were organized all over the country, and military officials began to mutiny. The revolutionaries formed an alliance and established the Derg, a military-based committee that removed Haile Selassie and his cabinet from office in September 1974. Sixty former leaders were executed, and the leaders of the coup declared a new socialist state in Ethiopia. Haile Selassie was kept under house arrest and died the following year.

The leader of the new military-run communist government was Mengistu Haile Mariam. Many people who had objected to the monarchy also challenged this government, wanting instead a civilian government. This led to what is known as the Red Terror, during which the military flexed its power by executing approximately one hundred thousand Ethiopians, mostly students, and persecuting many more. Despite this violence, groups continued to protest the regime, and it was widely criticized. Meanwhile, the country was suffering in other ways.

Famine

In the early 1980s, a severe famine struck Ethiopia, in part because of drought and in part because of government policies that made it hard for people to supplement their incomes. At least four hundred thousand died. In response to the famine, the government moved six hundred thousand families from the north to the west and the south, where more land was supposed to be available. The people who were resettled were not given the food or tools they needed to start again. Suffering continued, and many people returned to their home villages. Over time, the famine, declining support from foreign communist powers, and ethnic-based rebellion all contributed to the Derg's downfall.

A young woman brandishes a gun in 1978, the time of the Red Terror, when the government was persecuting opposition forces.

More Recent Times

In 1991, the Ethiopian People's Revolutionary Democratic Front gained control of the capital city and forced Mengistu from the country. The following years were difficult, as the transitional government established control. In 1993 the government drafted a new constitution and granted Eritrea independence. The constitution was signed in 1994, and in 1995 Negasso Gidada became the first president, while Meles Zenawi took the role of prime minister.

Meanwhile, Eritrea was dissatisfied with the placement of the border, and smaller disputes between Ethiopia and Eritrea turned into a full-scale war in 1998. A cease-fire was signed in 2000, but not before over sixty thousand people had died in the conflict. The cease-fire established a no-weapons zone

The presidential palace burned in 1991, during the civil war that forced Mengistu Haile Mariam from power.

along the border, which lasted until 2008. Since then, the border has experienced small skirmishes, and it remains a volatile region. In 2006, Ethiopia became involved in military action against the Somali, and remained in conflict until 2009.

In recent years, Ethiopia has continued to struggle with ensuring basic human and democratic rights. Activists and journalists have been jailed, and protesters have been harassed and even shot. In 2018, the government released many prisoners who had been jailed for speaking out against government leaders. Such moves have given some Ethiopians hope that political reform may be possible.

Somali women and children at a refugee camp in eastern Ethiopia. More than a million refugees from nearby countries live in Ethiopia.

Birtukan Mideksa is greeted by supporters after her release from prison in 2010.

Fighting for Change

Some Ethiopians who have fought for political reform in their country have suffered severe consequences. Birtukan Mideksa was born in Addis Ababa. She studied law at Addis Ababa University and eventually became a judge. She quickly realized that the government did not follow the law and constitution, and she joined a political movement, known as the Coalition for Unity and Democracy, dedicated to making social change. In 2005, after her party lost the election, she was arrested on charges of attempting to overthrow the government. She was released in 2007, only to be arrested again in 2008 and sentenced to life in prison.

This caught the attention of human rights organizations such as Amnesty International. They started a campaign to have her released because she had not committed a crime, she had only disagreed with her government. She was finally released in 2010. She went on to earn a master's degree in public administration from Harvard University in Massachusetts.

CHAPTER 5

Governing a New Democracy

Although Ethiopia is among the oldest of nations, its democracy is new. After the government of Haile Selassie was overthrown in 1974 by the Ethiopian military, a communist government known as the Derg took power. That government was often tyrannical and a civil war led to its end in 1991. A transitional government took control, and Ethiopia adopted a new constitution in 1994. Elections to the new legislature were held in 1995, marking the beginning of the Federal Democratic Republic of Ethiopia.

Opposite: **The Lion of Judah is a symbol of Ethiopia. The statue was taken to Rome, Italy, when the Italian army occupied Ethiopia in the 1930s. It was not returned to Addis Ababa until the 1960s.**

The Structure of Government

Like many other governments, the national government of Ethiopia has three parts: the executive, legislative, and judicial branches. The 1994 constitution created a parliamentary

A New Anthem

The Ethiopian national anthem, "March Forward, Dear Mother Ethiopia," was adopted in 1992 after the fall of Ethiopia's communist government. The anthem was written by Dereje Melaku Mengesha and composed by Solomon Lulu.

English translation

Respect for citizenship is strong in our Ethiopia;
National pride is seen, shining from one side to another.
For peace, for justice, for the freedom of peoples,
In equality and in love we stand united.
Firm of foundation, we do not dismiss humanness;
We are peoples who live through work.
Wonderful is the stage of tradition, mistress of proud heritage,
Mother of natural virtue, mother of a valorous people.
We shall protect you—we have a duty;
Our Ethiopia, live! And let us be proud of you!

Ethiopia's National Government

Executive Branch

President

Prime Minister

Council of Ministers

Legislative Branch

House of Peoples' Representatives (547 members)

House of Federation (153 members)

Judicial Branch

Supreme Court

High Courts

Courts of First Instance

In 2017, 39 percent of the members of Ethiopia's parliament were women.

The Center of the Nation

Addis Ababa, the capital of Ethiopia, is the third-highest capital city in the world, sitting at an elevation of about 8,000 feet (2,440 m) above sea level. This city of more than three million residents is located in the center of the country to the west of the Great Rift Valley.

Emperor Melenik II founded the city in 1886, and it became the nation's first permanent capital. Today, it is the center of trade, transportation, and industry in Ethiopia. Addis Ababa has the largest market in Africa. As the headquarters of the African Union, a political organization that includes all the nations in Africa, it is also the diplomatic center of the continent. Most residents of the city live in apartments and wear Western-style clothing.

The city is home to many important cultural institutions, including Addis Ababa University, the National Museum of Ethiopia, the Ethiopian Ethnological Museum, and the Ethiopian National Library. Other important sites include Holy Trinity Cathedral, a large Ethiopian Orthodox church where Emperor Haile Selassie is buried.

Addis Ababa means "New Flower" in the Amharic language.

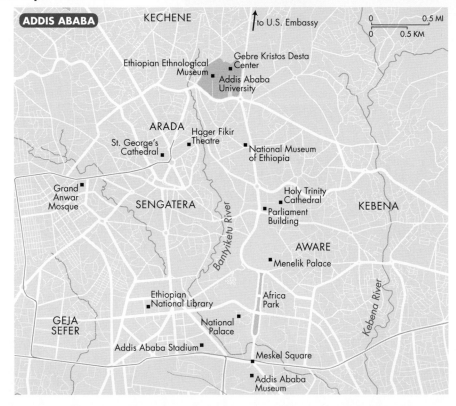

ADDIS ABABA

KECHENE

to U.S. Embassy

0   0.5 MI
0   0.5 KM

Ethiopian Ethnological Museum

Gebre Kristos Desta Center

Addis Ababa University

ARADA

Hager Fikir Theatre

St. George's Cathedral

National Museum of Ethiopia

Grand Anwar Mosque

SENGATERA

Bantyiketu River

Holy Trinity Cathedral

Parliament Building

KEBENA

AWARE

Menelik Palace

Kebena River

Ethiopian National Library

Africa Park

GEJA SEFER

National Palace

Addis Ababa Stadium

Meskel Square

Addis Ababa Museum

form of government, with each branch of government independent of the others.

Making Laws

The power to make laws is given to two legislative bodies, the House of Peoples' Representatives and the House of Federation. The House of Peoples' Representatives is the only body whose members are directly elected by the people. It has 547 members who are elected to five-year terms; voting districts are based on population.

The 153 members of the House of Federation are appointed by the legislatures of each of the nine states. Each state decides whether its representatives to the House of Federation are appointed by the State Council or elected by the people. Members of the House of Federation serve five-year terms.

Supporters wave the red flag of the ruling party, the Ethiopian People's Revolutionary Democratic Front, during a rally.

Carrying Out Laws

The president of the Federal Democratic Republic of Ethiopia is the head of state, the official representative of the country. Serving as president, however, is mostly a ceremonial job, and the president is not actively involved in running the government. The president is nominated by the House of Peoples' Representatives and must be approved by a two-thirds vote in both houses of parliament. Presidents can serve for two six-year terms.

Abiy Ahmed (right) became prime minister in 2018. He is the first prime minister from the Oromo community, the country's largest ethnic group.

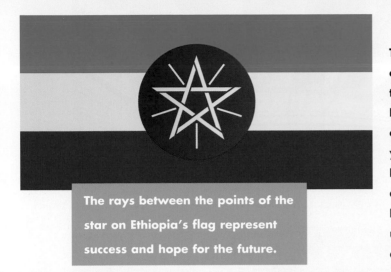

A Symbol of Unity

The Ethiopian flag has three horizontal stripes of green, yellow, and red. Green stands for the nation's fertile land and hope, yellow for harmony and justice, and red for the sacrifice of patriotism. In the center of the flag is a yellow star against a blue background. The blue represents peace, and the star symbolizes equality and the nation's bright future. The background of the Ethiopian flag has been in use since 1895, and the central design was added in 1996.

The rays between the points of the star on Ethiopia's flag represent success and hope for the future.

The real power in the Ethiopian government is held by the prime minister and the Council of Ministers. After an election, the House of Peoples' Representatives chooses the prime minister and other ministers who lead government departments. The prime minister is also head of the Ethiopian armed forces.

The current prime minister is Abiy Ahmed. He is a leader of the Oromo Peoples' Democratic Organization. It is one of several parties that together make up the Ethiopian People's Revolutionary Democratic Front (EPRDF), the coalition that has ruled Ethiopia since 1991.

Interpreting the Laws

In Ethiopia, courts are supposed to be independent of the legislative branch and executive branches of government. But in fact, the ruling party, the EPRDF, has significant control over the courts and the judicial system.

Ethiopia is a founding member of the African Union, an international organization that works to promote unity and economic development across the continent. The African Union's headquarters is in a modern building in Addis Ababa.

The federal (national) court system in Ethiopia consists of courts of first instance, where many trials begin. Trials can move up to the high courts and eventually to the Supreme Court. Each state has a similar system of courts.

The federal Supreme Court is the highest court in the land. It hears appeals of decisions from lower federal courts at the federal levels. It also hears appeals from state courts when federal issues are involved.

Some cases in Ethiopia are heard in Sharia courts. These courts try cases based on Islamic religious laws rather than on laws established by the legislatures. In Ethiopia, Sharia courts have to be officially established by the government, and they have to follow the same rules and procedures as federal and state courts. All the parties involved in a case must agree to have it heard in a Sharia court, or the case is transferred to a government court. Ethiopia currently has three federal Sharia courts as well as local Sharia courts.

State and Local Government

Ethiopia is divided into nine smaller units called states. The borders of these states were drawn based upon ethnicity, language, and settlement patterns. Because settlement patterns determined the borders, the state boundaries are irregular and their sizes vary greatly. The smallest, Harari, covers just 129 square miles (334 sq km), a fraction of the size of Rhode Island. The largest, Oromia, has an area of almost 110,000 square miles (285,000 sq km), larger than California and Pennsylvania combined.

Ethiopia has two chartered cities that do not lie within any state: the capital city of Addis Ababa, and the city of Dire Dawa.

Each state has its own government that deals with local issues. Like the national government, state governments have a legislative branch that enacts laws and regulations for the state, an executive branch that carries out those laws, and a judicial branch to ensure that the laws are followed.

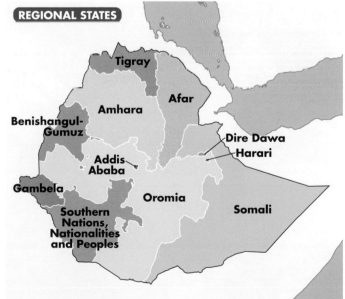

REGIONAL STATES

CHAPTER 6

A Growing Economy

E THIOPIA'S ECONOMY IS ONE OF THE FASTEST GROW-ing in the world. It's gross domestic product (GDP), the total value of the goods and services it produces, is increasing between 8 percent and 11 percent per year. To encourage this growth, the government is investing in infrastructure such as roads and rail lines and encouraging foreign businesses. This has produced huge growth in the construction industry. The service sector is also growing as transportation, communications, hotels, and trade expand. Despite this rapid growth, many Ethiopians are still in poverty. About 30 percent of Ethiopians live below the international poverty line.

Opposite: **Brightly colored baskets for sale at a market in Aksum. Selling goods is part of the service sector, the largest part of Ethiopia's economy.**

Agriculture

Agriculture, once the largest part of Ethiopia's economy, now contributes around 36 percent of the GDP. Most farming is

Working Abroad

In Ethiopia, unemployment sits at around 20 percent. Work is particularly difficult for younger people to find. Because of this, a large number of workers, especially young women, have moved to countries such as Saudi Arabia, Lebanon, and Oman to work. Most work as household servants. These jobs come with extremely low wages and long hours. Many employers have exploited these workers, especially those who are not working legally. The Ethiopian government has made several attempts to stop this, including enacting travel bans, ordering the return of Ethiopians working illegally in other countries, and regulating employment agencies that send workers to foreign countries. Still, the problem remains.

done on small plots of land no larger than 5 acres (2 hectares) and is worked by just one or two people. These small farms supply enough food for a single family. If there are crops left over, they are sold at markets to provide income for other needs. The most common crops are teff, wheat, corn, chickpeas, barley, beans, and oats.

Large-scale farms grow cash crops that are sold domestically and exported. The coffee industry is the largest export product, accounting for about a quarter of the country's total export earnings. Another 14 percent of revenue comes from oil-producing seeds like sesame. About 10 percent comes from khat, a plant with a stimulant effect that is widely used on the Arabian Peninsula but is illegal in many countries, including the United States and Canada.

Ethiopia has one of the largest livestock populations in all of Africa, with over fifty million head of cattle, thirty million sheep, and twenty million goats. A large portion of the country's livestock is kept by families, including some who migrate with their herds from waterhole to waterhole. Foreign investors have begun running factory farms to raise cattle,

Shepherds keep an eye on their flock in southern Ethiopia.

Workers at a plant in Mekele prepare honey for sale.

The Luck of the Bees

For thousands of years, bees have been a symbol of good luck in Ethiopia. They are also associated with royalty. Legend says that King Lalibela was surrounded by a swarm of bees at birth. His mother took this as a sign he would be king, so she named him Lalibela, meaning "the man bees obey."

Today in Ethiopia, honey can be found in almost every household. It has long been used for food and for medicinal purposes, used to treat wounds, stomach illnesses, and infections. Honey is also used to make an alcohol called *tej*, which is the national drink of Ethiopia.

The white honey of Tigray, in northern Ethiopia, is the most precious of Ethiopian honeys, unique in color and taste because of the blossom the bees feed on, which is a localized relative of the sage plant. This white honey is a highly prized delicacy admired around the world. Unfortunately, it is being threatened by climate change because the plants can survive only in low temperatures found at higher elevations.

but the lease agreements allow these to be exported without tax, so the farms provide little revenue for Ethiopia. Chickens are common in both cities and rural areas. They are kept for both eggs and meat. Beekeeping for honey and beeswax has long been a tradition for Ethiopians and is a modest source of income for many people.

Manufacturing

Ethiopia's major manufacturing centers are in and around its large cities, especially those located on busy transport routes. Products made in Ethiopia include textiles, footwear, leather, cement, and processed foods like coffee. In 2016, manufacturing accounted for 4.5 percent of the GDP and about 16 percent of exports. But large industrial parks are being constructed in central and southern Ethiopia, and transportation is improving, so this is expected to increase.

Small artisanal manufacturing of consumer goods is important for the domestic economy. These include products such

Factories in Ethiopia produce clothes for the Gap, H&M, and many other companies. The textile industry in Ethiopia is expanding rapidly.

as tools, furniture, rugs, baskets, pottery, jewelry, and other everyday items.

What Ethiopia Grows, Makes, and Mines

Agriculture

Oil Seeds (2016)	790,000 metric tons
Coffee (2017)	393,000 metric tons
Khat (2017)	1.2 million acres

Manufacturing (2016, value in exports)

Textiles	$94.1 million
Leather and leather products	$86.8 million
Footwear	$43.8 million

Mining (2016, value in exports)

Gold	$378 million
Precious stones	$15 million
Tantalum and niobium	$9.3 million

Natural Resources

Ethiopia's land holds many mineral resources, but most have not been developed as sources of income. Right now only about 1 percent of the GDP comes from natural resources.

Gold has been mined in Ethiopia for thousands of years. Today, there is one large commercial mine in the southern Oromia region. The mine produces as much as 10,000 pounds (4,500 kg) of mixed gold and silver ore per year.

This is exported to Switzerland and then refined to separate the metals, which are bought by Swiss banks. Plans are under way for creating additional gold mines in other parts of the country, and exports are likely to increase significantly.

Tantalum, which is a rare metal used in laboratory equipment and electronics such as cell phones, is mined in Kenticha in southern Ethiopia. This metal, which doesn't corrode, is often used in place of platinum, which is also mined in smaller quantities in the western parts of the country.

Commercial mining for potash, used in fertilizers, has begun to increase as the government makes it more attractive for foreigners to invest in Ethiopia. Copper, niobium, gypsum, cement, and soda ash are also mined commercially. Salt is the country's most accessible mineral, however it is harvested only on a small scale.

The land under Ethiopia also contains some gemstones. Typically, they are mined by individuals rather than companies. The miners sell the gems in their rough form. Opals are the most widely mined. Since 2013, they have become the focus of government regulations because they were being exported at prices far below market value. This happened because the miners knew little about how to grade the gems on their quality, and Ethiopia had few processing facilities to refine the opals before they were sold. As a result, millions of dollars of potential income for Ethiopians was lost. Since

White Gold

For centuries, the Afar people have mined salt from the floor of the Danakil Depression. At one time these thick slabs of salt were used as currency, called amole. Today, each salt brick is worth around 20 cents.

The miners today use the same technology that their ancestors did. Each day, they walk with their caravan of camels for hours to reach the jagged, parched salt deposits. They then use axes and hand tools to chop blocks from the thick crust, and pry them up with long sticks. At the end of the day, they load the bricks onto their camels' backs and make the long journey to Berhale, a salt-trading town at the edge of the desert. Because of

Miners cut the salt into standard-size blocks and then load them onto camels for transport to market.

the difficult conditions and other options for work, the number of Afar salt miners has declined.

Foreign investors from the United States and other countries once engaged in commercial mining of the expansive salt deposits in the Danakil Depression. They stopped because of the harsh conditions and low profit margins. As the Ethiopian government continues to encourage foreign investors, large-scale mining is once again being considered for this area. The ongoing conflict with bordering Eritrea is now the biggest obstacle to these plans.

Men chop chunks of salt from the earth in the Danakil Depression.

then, the government has required that a percentage of the opals exported be cut and polished. By 2017, half of all opals exported from Ethiopia had to be finished.

Other Ethiopian gemstones mined include garnet, amethyst, sapphire, tourmaline, and aquamarine. None of these contribute greatly to the economy.

Energy

Ethiopia's powerful rivers are a valuable resource because they produce hydroelectric power. The Blue Nile, Awash, Shebele, Omo, and Gilgel Gibe Rivers all have dams that harness power from running water.

The Grand Ethiopian Renaissance Dam is being constructed on the Blue Nile in northern Ethiopia. When complete, it will be the biggest dam in Africa.

Ninety percent of the nation's power comes from hydro-electricity, which is a clean and renewable source. But its use is limited to those within the reach of established power grids, which do not carry the electricity everywhere throughout the country. The Grand Ethiopian Renaissance Dam being built on the Blue Nile will contribute a significant amount of power once complete, but additional power plants will be needed to provide power to the bulk of the rural population. The dam, however, has sparked controversy with Egypt, which is highly dependent on the flow of water from the Blue Nile.

An Oromo woman carries firewood home.

Only 24 percent of the people have access to electricity. This means most of the population has no refrigeration to

Enchantment of the World Ethiopia

The 1-birr note depicts a young boy on the front.

Money Facts

The Ethiopian birr is the official currency of Ethiopia. Each birr is divided into one hundred santim. Coins come in denominations of 5, 10, 25, and 50 santim, and 1 birr. Paper currency is made in values of 1, 5, 10, 50, and 100 birr. The banknotes depict images of national pride and history, including Tissisat Falls, coffee, the Enqulal Gemb fortress at Gondar, farming, and basket weaving. In 2018, 28 birr equaled $1.

keep food safe in the heat, no electric appliances, and no air-conditioning to get relief from high temperatures.

Wood is the primary energy source for many Ethiopians. For those living in rural areas, wood is often the only energy source. As a result, many forests have been cut down. Deforestation is a threat to many people. Without trees to hold the soil in place, the wind and water can easily carry it away.

Trade

In 2016, Ethiopia's exports, the goods sold outside the country, were valued at $2.9 billion. Among Ethiopia's largest export partners is Switzerland, which buys nearly all the gold that is mined in Ethiopia. Other important trading partners are China, Saudi Arabia, Germany, and the United States. Coffee accounts for one-third of export revenue, while oil seeds and khat exports contribute another one-third. Gold exports make up about 17 percent, and fresh flowers and small animals each account for 7 percent.

Ethiopia imports, or brings into the country, far more goods than it exports. Refined metals and machinery, including motor vehicles and aircraft, each make up 24 percent of imports, while electronic equipment accounts for 13 percent. Fertilizers, chemicals, and products made from oil make up approximately 14 percent of imports.

The Ethiopian government is also aggressively leasing land to foreign investors to encourage them to build factories and farms. In Ethiopia, the government owns all of the land, which it leases to people and businesses. The rates offered to foreign investors average $2.60 per acre ($6.55 per hectare), which is

Bags of coffee are piled high in a warehouse in Addis Ababa, ready to be exported.

Enchantment of the World Ethiopia

Farmers weigh coffee beans for sale.

How Much?

Ethiopia adopted the metric system in 1963, but many Ethiopians continue to use traditional units for everyday household measurements. The names and metric equivalents vary a great deal depending on the region and often on who is doing the measuring, especially for distances that are based on body parts! Here are a few examples:

Length

Kend = the distance from the tip of the middle finger to the tip of the elbow

Sinzir = the distance from the tip of the thumb to the tip of the middle finger when the hand is spread wide

Chamma = the distance from the tip of the big toe to the back of the heel

Ermijja = the length of a long step

Volume

Enqib = approximately one bushel, used to measure harvested crops like grains and coffee

Tassa (dry) = approximately 2 pounds (1 kg)

Kuba (wet) = approximately 1 quart (1 liter)

Medeb = a bag of vegetables

Esir = a bundle of firewood or grass

drastically lower than the international average. Ethiopia also offers investors other benefits, including deferred taxes, cheap energy, inexpensive labor, and a complete lack of restrictions on what they may do with their products. These policies are receiving growing criticism within Ethiopia.

Going Places

One of Ethiopia's greatest economic challenges is its infrastructure. Access to power, communications, and efficient transportation are all needed to develop and expand busi-

A light rail system opened in Addis Ababa in 2015, connecting the city center to outlying areas.

ness and trade. As of 2015, only 15 percent of the nation's roads were paved, and the long-deteriorated Djibouti–Addis Ababa railway was still being repaired. In 2016, a new electric railway opened. The single 409-mile (658 km) line reaches from the Djibouti border to the capital city. Of the country's seventy-seven airports, only seventeen have paved runways, and just three of these are large enough to accommodate large jets. There is one state-owned airline that operates all air travel within the country.

Communications systems are limited in Ethiopia, including landline telephones, internet service, and cell

Ethiopians take a selfie in front of a castle in Gondar. About half the people in Ethiopia have cell phones.

phones. The Ethiopian government owns all telecommunications and has been trying to lower costs and expand service. In 2016, about half the population had cell phones. Service is limited, and even charging phones can be difficult for those in rural areas without access to electricity. Only 15 percent of the population has internet service.

CHAPTER 7

A United People

THE PEOPLE OF ETHIOPIA TAKE PRIDE IN THEIR diversity. Dozens of ethnic groups, both large and small, have worked together over the centuries to maintain the nation's independence from foreign rule. Even with differences in language and traditions, these groups live side by side in relative peace. Despite their own problems of drought, famine, and poverty, the nation welcomes refugees from neighboring countries whose homelands are violent and oppressive.

Opposite: **People from the Oromo ethnic group attend a festival in Addis Ababa. The capital is a diverse city, with no one ethnic group making up a majority of the population.**

Where Ethiopians Live

As of 2017, Ethiopia has a population of approximately 105,350,000, the second highest in Africa, with a growth rate of just under 3 percent. If the country's population continues to increase at this pace, it will double by 2060. Only about 20 percent of Ethiopians live in or near cities, while

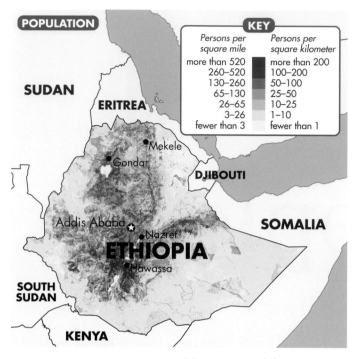

KEY	
Persons per square mile	Persons per square kilometer
more than 520	more than 200
260–520	100–200
130–260	50–100
65–130	25–50
26–65	10–25
3–26	1–10
fewer than 3	fewer than 1

SUDAN

ERITREA

Mekele

Gondar

DJIBOUTI

Addis Ababa

Nazret

SOMALIA

ETHIOPIA

Hawassa

SOUTH SUDAN

KENYA

Population of Major Cities

Addis Ababa

3,273,000

Nazret 324,000

Gondar 323,900

Mekele 323,700

Hawassa 300,100

the remaining 80 percent reside in rural areas. The most populated areas are in the Upper Rift Valley and the Western Highlands, where the climate is the most moderate and the land is good for farming.

People living in rural areas tend to build near their farms or are grouped with others in small villages. Most rural homes are built by hand from wood plastered with a mixture of mud and straw and have thatched roofs. These are often round, with a cone-shaped roof. Newer rural homes sometimes use corrugated steel for roofing, which requires a rectangular building.

Health

Ethiopia has one of the lowest life expectancies in the world. Women live an average of sixty-five years, and men just sixty years. One of the biggest health threats in Ethiopia is malnutrition, which can make the people more likely to be sickened by viruses and infections because their bodies are not strong enough to fight them off. Major droughts since 2013 have left a much larger percentage of the population, particularly in the dry eastern region, undernourished and without clean water. Waterborne disease is common because many people do not have access to fresh water.

Ethiopia has one of the lowest doctor-patient ratios in the world. There is only one doctor for about every thirty thousand patients. The only fully equipped hospitals are in major cities, with the largest located in Addis Ababa. Smaller part-time clinics are scattered in populated rural areas. Most Ethiopians, however, rely on traditional plant-based medicine. International organizations like Doctors Without Borders do what they can to bring aid to the most needy areas. Thanks to the work of many nongovernmental organizations as well as efforts by the Ministry of Health, the immunization rate for children is now up to 70 percent.

A farmer and his family work in a field of teff. Ethiopian families have an average of 4.2 children.

The Suri People

The Suri, a subgroup of the Surma, live in southwestern Ethiopia on the plains of the Great Rift Valley near the South Sudan border. Grazing large herds of cattle is their main livelihood. Suri clans, extended family groups, sometimes clash with each other over grazing land.

Young Suri men have traditionally gathered in groups for a ritualized fight called Donga, which is a way for them to impress potential wives. Groups from different clans will meet for the celebratory event and fight with sticks. Even though the fighting is ritualized, it can sometimes be deadly. The Ethiopian government banned stick fighting in 1994, but it is still practiced.

Suri women impress future suitors with face and body paint, elaborate headdresses, and scarification. These are considered forms of self-expression and beauty.

Another custom is wearing lip plates, which indicate a woman's value in marriage. When a girl comes of age, two bottom teeth are removed and a hole is made in her bottom lip, which is then gradually stretched using wooden discs of increasing size.

A Land of Diverse Peoples

Ethiopia is an ethnically diverse nation with a long history of many groups living together peacefully. The largest groups are the Oromo and the Amhara. The Oromos live in the central and southwestern regions, while the Amharas occupy the central highlands. Beyond the languages and traditions of major ethnic groups, each group and region has its own set of cultural and social rules.

The Afar peoples account for only 1.7 percent of the population, but their region is quite large, occupying almost all of

An elderly Oromo woman. More than one in three Ethiopians is Oromo.

Ethiopia's Ethnic Groups	
Oromo	34.5%
Amhara	26.9%
Somali	6.2%
Tigray	6.1%
Sidama	4.0%
Gurage	2.5%
Welaita	2.3%
Afar	1.7%
Hadiya	1.7%
Gamo	1.5%
Gedeo	1.3%
Other	8.8%

the Danakil Depression. It is the extreme hot climate of the Danakil Desert that has kept other groups out for the past one thousand years. The Afar people have adapted to the conditions and need far less water to survive than the average person does. They are nomadic, traveling with herds of goats and camels. Some harvest salt slabs by hand for income.

Many Different Languages

Ethiopia's official language is Amharic, a Semitic language distantly related to Arabic and Hebrew. Although it is the official language, only around 30 percent of Ethiopians consider it their primary language. More than a third of Ethiopians speak Oromo, the official language for the state of Oromia, which spreads west and south from the central region of the Great Rift Valley. The states of Somali, Tigray, and Afar also have their own official languages. In total, more than a hundred languages are used in Ethiopia, most of them isolated to specific ethnic groups. The home languages of refugees are spoken in their own communities, and many children now also learn basic English in school.

The Amharic language has its own script, or alphabet. Each character is called a *fidel*. There are thirty-three different consonants, each of which can be written seven different ways. How each fidel is written depends on the vowel sound that accompanies it.

More than one system is used to convert Amharic fidel script into the Latin alphabet used in English. This is why the names of towns and phrases may have more than one spelling.

Common Amharic Phrases

Tenaistellen	Hello (formal)
Salam	Hello (informal)
Yikirta	Excuse me
Abakish	Please
Amasagganallahu	Thank you
Minim aydallam	You're welcome
Awo	Yes
Aye	No

A girl studies English in school in Lalibela.

CHAPTER 8

Spiritual Cooperation

ETHIOPIA'S POPULATION IS ABOUT TWO-THIRDS Christian and one-third Muslim, with a very small Jewish community and a few isolated groups that follow African traditional religion. About 65 percent of the Christians belong to the Ethiopian Orthodox Church, a unique Christian faith that has retained some elements of its Jewish roots. Like the nation's various ethnic groups, Ethiopia's different religions have a history of living together in mutual respect.

Judaism and Early Christianity

Before the introduction of Christianity, many people living in what is now northern Ethiopia had been followers of Judaism for over a thousand years. It is widely believed that Menelik I, the legendary son of King Solomon and the Queen of Sheba,

Opposite: **Members of the Ethiopian Orthodox Church take part in a procession during Easter.**

Religion in Ethiopia	
Ethiopian Orthodox	43.1%
Muslim	34.1%
Protestant	19.4%
African traditional religion	1.5%
Roman Catholic	0.9%
Other	1%

brought Judaism to the empire. This belief arises from the creation of the national epic, called the *Kebra Negast*, which dates to the ninth century CE—well after the reputed meeting of King Solomon and the Queen of Sheba.

The conversion to Christianity happened in the fourth century during the rule of emperor Ezana of the Aksumite Kingdom. Missionaries from Antioch, in what is now Turkey, were traveling to India when they were shipwrecked on the coastline of what is now Eritrea. They were escorted to the capital city of Aksum, where they introduced the Ethiopian people to Christianity. The emperor adopted the new religion

An Ethiopian Orthodox priest reads a bible written in Amharic.

Saint Frumentius

Legend credits a man named Frumentius with the Aksumite conversion to Christianity. The story says that he and his brother were shipwrecked. They were brought to the king and enslaved. Over time they gained the king's respect and were asked to teach his children, including the future Emperor Ezana. After they were released from slavery, Frumentius traveled to Alexandria, Egypt, and asked the head of the church, Athanasius, to send a bishop and missionaries back to the Aksumites to spread the religion. Athanasius decided that he would ordain Frumentius as bishop instead and put him in charge of the mission.

When Frumentius returned to Ethiopia, he established the seat of the church in Aksum and converted Emperor Ezana. Frumentius became the first Archbishop of the Ethiopian Church, and he is believed to have been the first person to translate the New Testament of the Bible into Ge'ez, the language of the Aksumites.

Ethiopians used the title *abuna*, meaning "our father," when talking to Frumentius. This title is still used for the leader of the Ethiopian Orthodox Church.

Frumentius was born in Tyre, a city on the Mediterranean, in what is now Lebanon.

to help secure a good relationship with the prosperous Roman Empire. It was declared the official religion in 330 CE, and formed the roots of the Ethiopian Orthodox Church.

Timket, the largest festival in Ethiopia, recalls the baptism of Jesus. As part of the festival, some people reenact the event by swimming in the historic baths at Gondar.

The Ethiopian Orthodox Church

The Ethiopian Orthodox Church, called Tewahedo in Ethiopia, is one of the oldest established Christian churches anywhere in the world. It was the official religion of the Ethiopian Kingdom until 1974, and it remains the religion of more than 40 percent of Ethiopians.

The faith's roots are deep in the Old Testament, and because of this the church has many rules that are similar to Judaism. Among these are restrictions on foods, including restrictions on which days meat is allowed. Meat is forbidden on more than half the days of the year, resulting in a lot of Ethiopian cooking being vegetarian.

The Ark of the Covenant

The Ethiopian Orthodox Church claims that it possesses the true Ark of the Covenant, the resting place of the original Ten Commandments on the stone slabs that God is said to have given to Moses in the Old Testament of the Bible. Legend says that King Menelik I was the son of the Queen of Sheba and King Solomon of Jerusalem, the original keeper of the Ark of the Covenant. The story says that when he was around twenty years old he went to meet his father and stayed for several years. During this time, Zadok, the high priest of the temple of Jerusalem and the keeper of the Ark, had a dream that Menelik should bring the Ark home with him to Ethiopia. When Menelik began his trip home, Zadok replaced the original with a fake and smuggled the true Ark out. By the time it was discovered, Solomon had also dreamed

A woman prays outside a chapel said to house the Ark of the Covenant.

that his son should have it with him, but commanded everyone who knew about the theft to keep it secret. This story is recorded in the national epic, the *Kebra Negast*.

According to the Bible, the Ark is a rectangular box about 4 feet long, 2.5 feet wide, and 2.5 feet tall (120 cm x 80 cm x 80 cm), topped by a heavy golden lid adorned with angels. The Ethiopian Orthodox Church claims that the Ark rests in a chapel at the Church of Our Lady Mary of Zion in the city of Aksum, where it is guarded night and day. The only person allowed to see it is the Guardian of the Ark. The Guardian is appointed for life and is not allowed to leave the chapel grounds once he has been appointed. Even the head of the Ethiopian Orthodox Church is not allowed to view the Ark.

Religious groups and historians worldwide have many theories about possible locations of the Ark of the Covenant, and many cultures claim to have it. None, however, has been proved.

An Ethiopian Orthodox priest carries a copy of the Ark of the Covenant during a festival.

Religious Towns and Treasures

Ethiopia has many important religious sites where people go on pilgrimages. The churches of Lalibela are some of the most spectacular sights in the world. Instead of being built from the ground up, the red volcanic rock was carved away, leaving a solid stone rising from a deep hole. The windows, doors, and rooms were then carved from the rock until it was a full building with floors, steps, and decorative carvings. There are eleven rock churches in Lalibela, many of which are connected by tunnels carved from one church to the next.

Pilgrims visit the Church of St. George in Lalibela. The church was carved from stone in the 1100s or 1200s.

The monasteries on Lake Tana's islands hold some of the oldest Ethiopian Orthodox Church relics. At one time, more than two dozen monasteries and churches were active on the islands, and several are still operating today. The small monastery of Tana Cherkos reputedly hid the Ark of the Covenant to prevent it from being stolen. The monastery of Daga Estefanos, built in the sixteenth century, has the mummified remains of five Ethiopian emperors on display in glass coffins. Many of these churches can be visited by tourists, however some do not allow women on the grounds due to old religious customs.

Screens create a walkway around Ura Kidane Meret, a fourteenth-century church on Lake Tana.

The Welcoming of Islam

During the seventh century CE, early Muslims, followers of the Prophet Muhammad, were being persecuted in Mecca, in what is now Saudi Arabia. When this was occurring, King Armah of the Aksumite Empire welcomed them as refugees. King Armah was widely known for his fairness and commitment to treating his subjects equally. Muhammad himself praised him for welcoming the Muslim refugees and urged his followers to live peacefully with their Christian neighbors. This set the tone for peaceful coexistence between Christians and Muslims in Ethiopia. With few exceptions, this has

The Qur'an, the holy book of Islam, states that Muslims should dress modestly. As a result, many Muslims, including these Ethiopian girls, cover their hair.

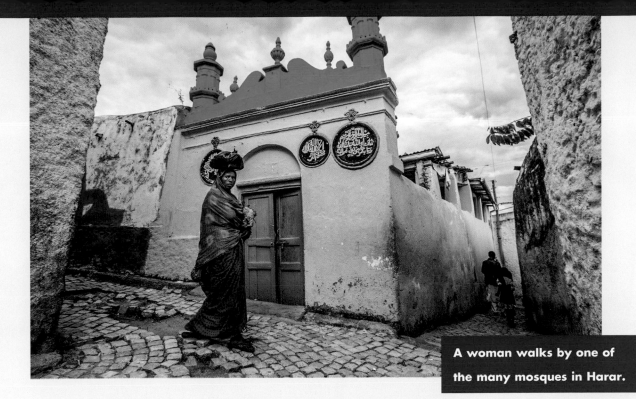

A woman walks by one of the many mosques in Harar.

City of Mosques

The city of Harar in eastern Ethiopia is considered one of the holiest cities in Islam. The city was founded in 1007 CE. The old part of the city is surrounded by thick 16.5-foot-tall (5 m) walls that were built between the thirteenth and sixteenth centuries. Within the walls, the city covers less than half a square mile (1 sq km), yet it is home to more than a hundred mosques amid its maze of narrow alleys.

This city is also known for its relationship with hyenas. Each evening, volunteers skewer meat on the ends of sticks. They hold the sticks in their mouths and feed the meat to wild hyenas. The hyenas' acceptance of food is considered a good omen, and the people live peacefully side by side with these notoriously deadly creatures.

helped the nation avoid religious battles that have arisen in other countries. The Muslim population in Ethiopia today is concentrated in the Eastern Lowlands, with smaller communities spread throughout the country. More than a third of Ethiopians identify as Muslim.

CHAPTER 9

Arts and Culture

THE OLDEST ART FOUND IN ETHIOPIA IS ROCK ART. Thousands of years ago, people began painting or etching images onto rocks and the walls of cliffs and caves. They depicted animals such as cattle and geometric symbols.

Around a thousand years ago, at Tiya, in the central part of the country, people erected a large group of stone monuments, called stelae. Many of the stelae feature intricate engravings, often of swords. Others depict humans. Experts have not yet determined which culture created this site.

Christian Art

Much of the earliest Ethiopian art to survive is closely tied to the Ethiopian Orthodox Church, which has been the major religion in Ethiopia for more than fifteen centuries. Many early churches still stand. They feature Biblical scenes and

Opposite: **A woman plays a large, double-headed kebero drum at a festival.**

An Ancient Art Workshop

In a cave in eastern Ethiopia, archaeologists have discovered a stash of more than four thousand pieces of ochre, a material used as a pigment to make rock art. Forty thousand years ago, people brought ochre to the cave. There it was chipped into small crayon-like pieces or ground into powders that were used for painting. Ochre contains iron and is usually a reddish color, but powders ranging from yellow to orange to gray have been found in the cave. Researchers have determined that early Ethiopians processed ochre in the cave for more than four thousand years.

pictures of saints, called icons, painted on the walls. Crosses were made in decorative metalwork, and pages of the Bible and other religious writings were illustrated in colored drawings and fancy lettering. These early works—some of which date back a thousand years—were all greatly influenced by the art of the Coptics, Christians who lived in Egypt. Coptic art followed the style of the Byzantine Church, based in Turkey. Most of the art was produced in monasteries, where monks illustrated manuscripts and made icons for the religious leaders, nobles, and rulers who supported the monasteries.

Why the Large Eyes?

The first thing you notice about early Ethiopian religious paintings is that most figures have large, wide-open eyes. Art historians call this the "reversal gaze." This idea holds that people don't just look at paintings, but that the paintings observe them as well. The saints are shown gazing intently back at the viewers in order to get their undivided attention. For this reason, sinful characters are not painted looking directly at the viewers. Instead they are often shown in profile with only one eye visible.

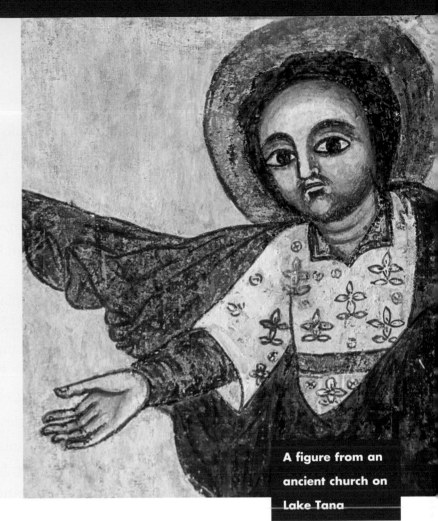

A figure from an ancient church on Lake Tana

This continued until the 1500s, when Muslims invaded Ethiopia and destroyed many churches. After the Muslim forces were driven out, the churches were rebuilt, but the art in them had a different style. It exhibited European influences because of the presence of Portuguese troops and missionaries. Still, it kept its Ethiopian character, depicting people with unusually large eyes, painted in strong, bright colors. Saints and other figures are drawn simply and in two dimensions, so they appear flat, and they are outlined in clear, bold lines. This kind of painting is still common in Ethiopian church art today.

A New Kind of Art

Other Ethiopian art uses a wide variety of styles. In the twentieth century, the government wanted to encourage cultural growth, so it brought in artists from around the world to work with local art students. A variety of artistic styles began to emerge, from traditional portraits, landscapes, and village scenes to abstract paintings and works that depicted a wider range of themes.

The biggest boost to Ethiopia's art scene came in 1958 with the opening of Haile Selassie I University's Alle School of Fine Arts and Design. Not only could students learn techniques here, but they could study the history of their own country's art and learn about art traditions elsewhere. Ethiopia's only art school, and one of the oldest in East Africa, Alle School has trained and influenced most of the well-known artists in the country today. Its founder, a prominent artist named Alle Felegeselam, was determined that the school would not be associated with any one artistic style. In 2010, the school merged with theater and music schools to become the College of Performing and Visual Arts.

Today, many of Ethiopia's promising young artists remember their country's long art history and lean toward local themes in their paintings. Their colorful works can be found in leading galleries far beyond Addis Ababa. Today, artists find a ready market for their work both in Ethiopia and abroad. Several galleries in Addis Ababa show and sell to local collectors and to tourists visiting the city. Foreign visitors look for paintings of traditional scenes of busy markets, churches,

Afewerk Tekle created stained glass windows for the Africa Hall at the headquarters for the United Nations Economic Commission for Africa in Addis Ababa.

Afewerk Tekle: Artist and Sculptor

Afewerk Tekle grew up in Ethiopia under the Italian occupation before and during World War II. He was determined to help rebuild his country by becoming a mining engineer. But while he was studying in England, his teachers saw his talent for art and encouraged him to study painting, sculpture, and architecture. He later learned to work with stained glass.

Tekle's reputation grew as he was commissioned to create mosaics and murals in St. George's Cathedral in Addis Ababa, the huge statue of Ras Makonnen in Harar, and several designs for postage stamps. Some of his work reflects his support for the decolonization movement to regain Africa from European colonialism. He died in 2012, at the age of eighty, as Ethiopia's best-known and most respected artist of his time.

and women preparing coffee, while local collectors and international galleries prefer more unconventional themes and abstract paintings.

Addis Ababa's modern art museum, the Gebre Kristos Desta Center, is dedicated to Ethiopia's emerging art scene. The center encourages and exhibits works that show creativity and experimentation in techniques, styles, and materials.

The museum is named for Gebre Kristos Desta, a modern artist who died in 1981 and who introduced modernism to Ethiopia. The gallery was designed by another prominent artist, Ethiopian architect Fasil Giorghis, and houses a permanent collection of Gebre Kristos Desta's paintings along with changing exhibits of modern art.

Popular arts are also an important part of Ethiopian life. People decorate everyday objects and clothing. Because of the many different ethnic groups in Ethiopia, these traditions vary greatly from place to place, and styles overlap with those of

An artist in Lalibela paints pictures in the traditional Ethiopian style.

neighboring African nations. Coiled baskets are made in rural regions and are used for carrying goods as well as for storing grains and beans. These baskets are often colorful, with designs worked into the wrapping that holds the coils together. The Muslim city of Harar is famous for its beautiful baskets.

Music

Ethiopia has a wide variety of music traditions. This is because each of the many ethnic groups has its own sounds and rhythms. Ethiopia's various religious traditions also add musical variety.

Whatever the ethnic group, folk songs are well-loved. Singing is popular at celebrations such as weddings, and it is often accompanied by dancing. Dance styles differ, too. Many people in the northern part of the country perform a dance called *eskista*, which means "dancing shoulders." This style is more about moving the neck and shoulders than the feet. In the center and south, the Oromo people dance with their whole body, with a lot of jumping, and the Gurage dance style is acrobatic.

A potter at work in Gondar

Karo men dance by jumping in the air. The jumps become higher as the dance progresses.

In rural areas, some music is performed by musicians called *azmaris*, who travel from village to village. In some places the azmaris invent verses, often based on some local person or event, and accompany the songs on a *masenqo*, a one-stringed instrument, that is played by rubbing a one-stringed bow against it. The masenqo is especially popular in the highlands, although it's played all over Ethiopia. Other instruments common in Ethiopia include the *begena*, a kind of small harp. It is used mostly to accompany Orthodox Christian hymns and spiritual music. The *washint* is a bamboo flute with four to six holes that is played with one hand. Washints were traditionally used by shepherds, but performers now play them. Because the washint is easy to learn, children often play it, too. Drums are also common in Ethiopian music. The *kebero* is a double-headed drum. A large kebero is used in Orthodox Christian music.

New and Old Mix

While Ethiopians play and listen to popular music, most prefer to listen to a mix of pop and traditional music. Most musicians play and sing both. Old and new styles exist side by side and often blend. One of the most influential Ethiopian musicians is Mulatu Astatke, whose innovative jazz has brought Ethiopian music to world attention. He blends traditional Ethiopian sounds with jazz, Afro-funk soul, and Latin music.

Women play begenas at an Ethiopian Orthodox festival. The instrument is played by plucking the strings.

The Father of Ethio-Jazz

Mulatu Astatke, who was born in Jimma in western Ethiopia in 1943, did not plan on a career in the arts. Instead, he went to England to study engineering, and only then discovered that his true passion was music. He stayed in London to study classical music at Trinity College, where he worked with British jazz artists as well as other African students who were introducing African music to Europe. He wanted to learn more about jazz, while also promoting Ethiopia's unique music.

The interests blended during his studies at Berklee College of Music in Boston, Massachusetts, where he began composing music that combined traditional Ethiopian music and sounds with Western rhythms and jazz. This so-called Ethio-jazz took Astatke to New York in the 1960s. There he founded the Ethiopian Quartet. He began traveling between the United States and Ethiopia, introducing this new style of music to people in both countries. Other musicians such as singer Mahmoud Ahmed and saxophonist Getatchew Mekurya picked up the cause of Ethio-jazz and helped change the musical scene in Ethiopia. By the beginning of the twenty-first century, Ethio-jazz hit the international scene. It remains popular, and Mulatu Astatke remains at the center of it.

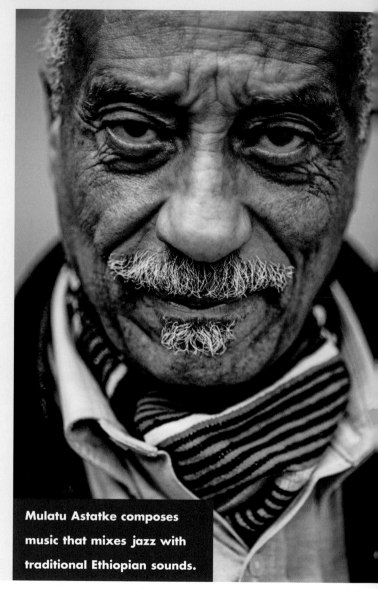

Mulatu Astatke composes music that mixes jazz with traditional Ethiopian sounds.

Guitarist Girum Mezmur and his Addis Acoustic Renaissance Group, along with the jazz band the Nubian Arc, perform at clubs in Addis Ababa. The best known

ambassadors of Ethiopian music internationally today are Teddy Afro, Aster Aweke, and the singer Gigi, who performs with major jazz musicians. Teddy Afro is known for bringing reggae influences into Ethiopian music.

Aster Aweke has been performing professionally since the 1970s. She has more than two dozen albums to her name.

Early Writing

Many different languages are spoken in Ethiopia. Over the years, two main languages, Ge'ez and Amharic, gained prominence. Ge'ez was the classical language, spoken by priests, monks, and a few others. It is still the language used in Ethiopian Orthodox Church services even though only a limited number of people can understand it. By the 1200s, Amharic had become the language of the military and of rulers and political leaders, and it went on to be the modern official language of Ethiopia.

The earliest literature in Ethiopia consisted of translations of Biblical texts. Eventually, religious and historical accounts and poetry were also produced. Then, in the late 1800s, missionaries brought printing presses to the country, and books began to be published in the language more people could read: Amharic. Most books, however, were still religious or historical. Newspapers began to be published in the early 1900s.

Modern Literature

Though there wasn't much fiction in Ethiopia before the arrival of the printing press, people did tell stories. The first novel in Amharic, *Libb-waled tarik* (An Imagined Story), written in 1908 by Afawark Gabra Iyasus, exhibits this storytelling tradition in its tale of a girl dressed up as a boy. The nation's first major modern writer was an Ethiopian foreign minister, Hiruy Walde Selassie, who addressed social issues such as child marriage and the conflict between Ethiopian traditions and new ideas from Europe.

After World War II, the conflicts between old and new and between Ethiopian and European ways of life continued to be a theme for many writers. One of these was Girmachew Tekle Hawaryat, whose novel *Araya* tells of a peasant who goes to Europe for his education. Short stories by Taddasa Liban look at how old and new ideas conflict in Ethiopian society. These and other social issues were also explored by writers such as P'awlos Nyonyo and Mengistu Gedamu. Emperor Haile Selassie encouraged literature and all the arts. During his rule, Kebede Mikael wrote dramas in verse and biographies, Tekle Tsadik Mekuria wrote history books, and Makonnen Endalkachew wrote plays and novels.

Ethiopian writer Abraham Verghese, also a medical doctor, is considered one of today's major African voices. His novel *Cutting for Stone*, published in 2009, tells the story of two brothers during Ethiopia's military revolution. He has also written nonfiction books about his life as a doctor. All of his books have been international best sellers.

CHAPTER 10

Everyday Life

CUSTOMS CAN BE VERY DIFFERENT FROM PLACE TO place in Ethiopia because of the many cultures and backgrounds of the people who live there. But the biggest differences in day-to-day life are between people who live in rural areas and those who live in cities. While city dwellers go to work to make money to spend on food and shelter, country life is about meeting basic needs by farming and using the resources that are nearby.

Precious Water

In Ethiopia, clean water is not always available. People living in cities can find clean water for drinking and cooking more easily. But for people who live in rural areas, which amounts to four-fifths of the population, safe water is much more difficult to find. Over half do not have access to clean water, and

Opposite: **Beads are a central element in the jewelry worn by the Hamar people of southwestern Ethiopia.**

Most Ethiopians live in the countryside, and many must travel each day to collect water. They often carry it in jugs called jerricans.

some spend their entire day fetching water. If they are lucky, the water comes from a fresh spring, but often it is collected from rivers, streams, and sometimes puddles that are shared with wildlife. All of these sources have contaminants that can make people sick. It is usually women and children who collect the water using large jugs, which are very heavy when they are full. They carry these jugs either on their backs or on top of their heads.

Education

About half the people in Ethiopia can read and write. Public education is free and mandatory for ages seven through twelve. Despite this, many children are unable to go to school. Most children attend primary schools, but middle school and high school have lower enrollment. Many families need their children to work to earn wages, to help on the family farm, or to collect water. And for rural families, schools can be far from where they live. Also, public funding for schools is low, making it difficult to find teachers and the resources needed.

Addis Ababa is home to the country's first university, founded in 1950 as the University College of Addis Ababa. The capital city now has many other colleges and universities where students can earn degrees in fields such as medicine, law, social policy, and art. The cities of Dire Dawa, Hawassa, Bahir Dar, Mekele, and Jimma also have colleges and universities.

Injera is usually eaten with a variety of stews.

Food

The best-known Ethiopian food is flatbread called injera. Injera is made from the teff grain, a plant native to the country. The grain is made into a runny paste, fermented for a few days, and then cooked into a giant, thin pancake. This flat sourdough bread, which is a little spongy, is then used as a plate for the rest of the meal. To eat, a person rips off a piece of the injera and uses it to pick up lentils, vegetables, or pieces of meat in the center of the

bread. Dishes called *alechas* or *wats* are usually spicy, seasoned with a peppery spice mixture called *berbere*. Common ingredients in these dishes include lentils, chickpeas, hard-boiled eggs, fish, beef, goat, and lamb. Ethiopians also enjoy injera dipped in sauces or spread with ghee, a clarified butter.

Honey is an important ingredient because of its nutritional value, and it is found in most homes. The national beverage, *tej*, is a type of wine made from honey. Honey is also used to sweeten the country's favorite beverage, coffee, which both adults and children drink.

Ethiopians have a traditional coffee ceremony, which they use as a gesture of hospitality. The ritual of making and serving the coffee is also a treasured social time for friends and family. The fresh beans are roasted over charcoal and ground by hand with a mortar and pestle. They are then brewed in a traditional clay coffeepot.

Dessert is not traditional in Ethiopia, but many people enjoy a coffee—with a lot of sugar—after

Spris can be made with many different fruits, but they often include thick avocado at the bottom.

Spris

Spris are Ethiopian fruit smoothies. They are simple to make, gorgeous to look at, and delicious to drink. Have an adult help you with this recipe.

Ingredients

2 small avocados

½ cup water

1 tablespoon honey

1 lime

1 large mango

Directions

Put the avocado in a blender with the water, honey, and juice of half the lime. Blend until it is completely smooth. Divide the blended avocado between two glasses. Wash out the blender. Put the mango in the blender and puree it. Pour the blended mango on top of the avocado in each glass to make a bright yellow layer on top of the green avocado layer. Squeeze a wedge of lime onto each drink, and then enjoy. You'll probably need a spoon!

a meal. In Addis Ababa, people who want a snack sometimes go into a fruit and vegetable shop for a *spris*. These thick, colorful drinks are made of layers of different fruits.

Clothing

What people wear in Ethiopia depends on where they live, their religious and cultural backgrounds, and what is available to them. Those in hotter regions wear thinner cloth and some people wear very little clothing. People in the cooler highlands wrap up in thick capes to stay warm at night. The most typical traditional dress of the highlands is white cotton, while Muslims in Harar wear colorful patterned clothes. Cattle-herding groups often wear leather clothing, and some more remote groups use plants and animal skins to make decorative ceremonial costumes. In cities, many Ethiopians often wear Western-style clothing.

Hairstyles, decoration, and jewelry are also influenced by ethnic background and what materials are available. Karo and Geleb men use clay to hold feathers in their hair. Some women have intricately braided hair, and many Muslim women cover their heads. Jewelry is common among Ethiopians. Beads made of brightly colored glass and amber are used to decorate hair and clothing. Bracelets, anklets, and necklaces are popular, most often made of brass or copper but sometimes gold or silver.

Sports

The favorite sport in Ethiopia is soccer. Professional leagues are very popular entertainment in large cities. The nation also has a national basketball league, and boxing is popular in some areas.

An Ethiopian boy playing soccer

Ethiopians have long dominated in the Olympics in middle-distance and long-distance running. The first Ethiopian to win the gold in the Olympic marathon was Abebe Bikila, who set world records during the 1960 and 1964 Olympics. He was the first person to win the gold medal in the marathon in two consecutive Olympics. Haile Gebrselassie set more than twenty world records for distance running. He won Olympic gold medals twice in a row for the 10,000 meter race, in 1996 and 2000.

In 2008, Tirunesh Dibaba became the first woman to win a gold medal in the 5,000 meter and the 10,000 meter races in the same Olympic Games. As of 2018, she holds the women's world record for the 5,000 meter race. Her younger sister Genzebe Dibaba holds the world record in the 1,500 meter race. Never before have siblings held world records in running at the same time. With an older sister and a cousin who have also captured Olympic medals, they are often hailed as the fastest family on the planet.

Tirunesh Dibaba, one of the world's great distance runners, powers toward the finish line in a 5,000 meter race.

A priest lights a bonfire as part of an Ethiopian new year's celebration.

Keeping Time

Most countries, including the United States, use the Gregorian calendar, but Ethiopia is an exception. The Ethiopian calendar, also known as the Ge'ez calendar, has some big differences from the Gregorian calendar. It is a thirteen-month calendar, with twelve months lasting thirty days and a thirteenth with five or six days. The sixth day occurs in leap years. The new year in the Ethiopian calendar falls in September of the Gregorian calendar. In a typical year, the Ethiopian new year begins on September 11. In a leap year, it begins on September 12.

The number of the year is also different in the Ethiopian calendar. It is seven or eight years behind the Gregorian calendar because the Ethiopian Orthodox Church calculates the birth of Jesus differently.

Month Number	Name	Gregorian Calendar Start Date
1	Meskerem	September 11
2	Tikemet	October 11
3	Hidar	November 10
4	Tahesas	December 10
5	Tir	January 9
6	Yekatit	February 8
7	Megabit	March 10
8	Miyaza	April 9
9	Ginbot	May 9
10	Sene	June 8
11	Hamle	July 8
12	Nehase	August 7
13	Pagume	September 6

Celebrate

Throughout the year, Ethiopians celebrate a wide variety of holidays and festivals. Some are Muslim, some are Christian, some are neither. They all bring people together.

Ethiopian new year is celebrated in September. At this time of year, the rains are ending and flowers are blooming in the highlands. Children dress in new clothes and bring flowers to people in their villages.

Ramadan, the ninth month in the Islamic calendar, is the holiest time of year for Muslims. For all of Ramadan, Muslims fast during the day, avoiding food and water from sunup to sundown. At the end of Ramadan, Muslims celebrate Eid al-Fitr. In the morning, they attend large communal prayers. They then enjoy time with family. Muslim holidays fall on different days from year to year because the Islamic calendar is eleven days shorter than the Gregorian calendar.

In Ethiopia, Christmas is celebrated on January 7. Christians attend mass early in the morning. The service includes a grand procession in which the priest carries the church's *tabot*, a replica of the Ark of the Covenant, a box said to hold the original rock etched with the Ten Commandments. The priest leads a procession of people carrying candles around the church three times, as the church bells ring out. After church, people head home for a feast with family and friends.

Epiphany occurs about two weeks after Christmas. In Ethiopia, it is known as Timket and it celebrates the baptism of Jesus. Timket is the largest, most colorful festival in Ethiopia. During Timket, each tabot is removed from its church and

wrapped in velvet. The priest carries it through the streets, with bright umbrellas shading it and huge crowds of people following. The priests pray through the night, and a mass is performed by torchlight at about 2:00 a.m. At dawn, the priests sprinkle water on the people gathered there to recall Jesus's baptism. The priests then lead processions carrying the tabots back to their churches. Finally, the people disperse to enjoy the rest of the festival.

Colorful umbrellas dot the crowd during a procession on Timket.

Timeline

Ethiopian History

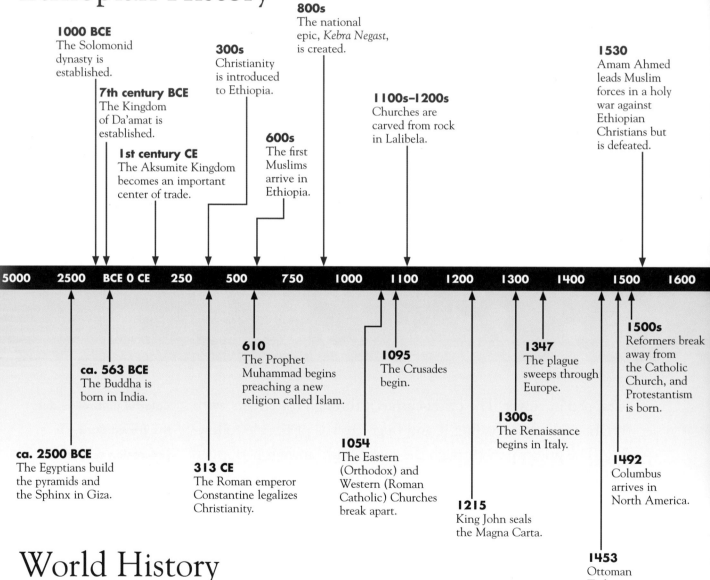

1000 BCE
The Solomonid dynasty is established.

7th century BCE
The Kingdom of Da'amat is established.

1st century CE
The Aksumite Kingdom becomes an important center of trade.

300s
Christianity is introduced to Ethiopia.

600s
The first Muslims arrive in Ethiopia.

800s
The national epic, *Kebra Negast*, is created.

1100s–1200s
Churches are carved from rock in Lalibela.

1530
Amam Ahmed leads Muslim forces in a holy war against Ethiopian Christians but is defeated.

5000	2500	BCE 0 CE	250	500	750	1000	1100	1200	1300	1400	1500	1600

ca. 2500 BCE
The Egyptians build the pyramids and the Sphinx in Giza.

ca. 563 BCE
The Buddha is born in India.

313 CE
The Roman emperor Constantine legalizes Christianity.

610
The Prophet Muhammad begins preaching a new religion called Islam.

1054
The Eastern (Orthodox) and Western (Roman Catholic) Churches break apart.

1095
The Crusades begin.

1215
King John seals the Magna Carta.

1300s
The Renaissance begins in Italy.

1347
The plague sweeps through Europe.

1453
Ottoman Turks capture Constantinople, conquering the Byzantine Empire.

1492
Columbus arrives in North America.

1500s
Reformers break away from the Catholic Church, and Protestantism is born.

World History

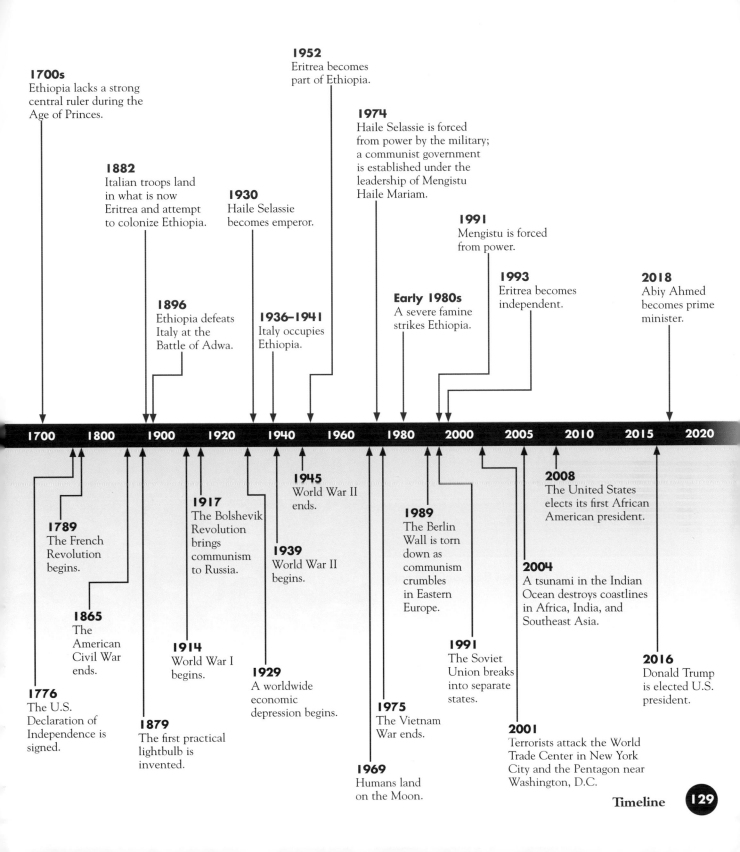

1700s
Ethiopia lacks a strong central ruler during the Age of Princes.

1882
Italian troops land in what is now Eritrea and attempt to colonize Ethiopia.

1930
Haile Selassie becomes emperor.

1952
Eritrea becomes part of Ethiopia.

1974
Haile Selassie is forced from power by the military; a communist government is established under the leadership of Mengistu Haile Mariam.

1991
Mengistu is forced from power.

1993
Eritrea becomes independent.

2018
Abiy Ahmed becomes prime minister.

1896
Ethiopia defeats Italy at the Battle of Adwa.

1936–1941
Italy occupies Ethiopia.

Early 1980s
A severe famine strikes Ethiopia.

| 1700 | 1800 | 1900 | 1920 | 1940 | 1960 | 1980 | 2000 | 2005 | 2010 | 2015 | 2020 |

1945
World War II ends.

2008
The United States elects its first African American president.

1789
The French Revolution begins.

1917
The Bolshevik Revolution brings communism to Russia.

1939
World War II begins.

1989
The Berlin Wall is torn down as communism crumbles in Eastern Europe.

2004
A tsunami in the Indian Ocean destroys coastlines in Africa, India, and Southeast Asia.

1865
The American Civil War ends.

1914
World War I begins.

1929
A worldwide economic depression begins.

1991
The Soviet Union breaks into separate states.

2016
Donald Trump is elected U.S. president.

1776
The U.S. Declaration of Independence is signed.

1879
The first practical lightbulb is invented.

1975
The Vietnam War ends.

2001
Terrorists attack the World Trade Center in New York City and the Pentagon near Washington, D.C.

1969
Humans land on the Moon.

Fast Facts

Official name:	Federal Democratic Republic of Ethiopia
Capital:	Addis Ababa
Official language:	Amharic
Official religion:	None
Year of founding:	1995
National anthem:	"March Forward, Dear Mother Ethiopia"
Type of government:	Federal democratic republic
Head of state:	President
Head of government:	Prime minister

Left to right: **National flag, political rally**

Gheralta Mountains

Area of country:	426,373 square miles (1,104,300 sq km)
Latitude and longitude of geographic center:	8°00' N, 38°00' E
Bordering countries:	South Sudan to the west, Sudan to the northwest, Eritrea to the north, Djibouti to the east, Somalia to the southeast, and Kenya to the south
Highest elevation:	Ras Dejen, 14,872 feet (4,533 m) above sea level
Lowest elevation:	Kobar Sink in the Danakil Depression, 410 feet (125 m) below sea level
Largest lake:	Tana, 1,418 square miles (3,673 sq km) in the rainy season
Average temperature extremes:	As low as 32°F (0°C) in the highlands, and as high as 116°F (47°C) in Dallol
Average annual precipitation:	Up to 80 inches (200 cm) in the southern Western Highlands; less than 20 inches (50 cm) in the Danakil Desert

National population (2017 est.):	105,350,000	
Population of major cities:	Addis Ababa	3,273,000
	Nazret	324,000
	Gondar	323,900
	Mekele	323,700
	Hawassa	300,100

Landmarks:
- ▶ *Churches of Lalibela*
- ▶ *Erta Ale lava lake,* Danakil Depression
- ▶ *Monasteries of Lake Tana Tissisat Falls (Blue Nile Falls),* Bahir Dar
- ▶ *Simien Mountains National Park,* near Gondar
- ▶ *Walled city of Harar*

Economy: Ethiopia's industry is dominated by the coffee and oil seed trades. Major manufacturing products include leather and leather goods, textiles, and processed meats. Mining contributes less to the economy, but the country has valuable metals like gold, silver, and tantalum, and gemstones like opals. The Ethiopian government is encouraging foreign investors to establish farms and factories in the country in hopes that it will boost the economy and industry overall.

Currency: Ethiopian birr. In 2018, 28 birr equaled $1.

System of weights and measures: Metric system

Literacy rate: 49%

Common Amharic words and phrases:		
	Tenaistellen	Hello (formal)
	Salam	Hello (informal)
	Yikirta	Excuse me
	Abakish	Please
	Amasagganallahu	Thank you
	Minim aydallam	You're welcome
	Awo	Yes
	Aye	No

Prominent Ethiopians:

Mulatu Astatke	(1943–)
Musician	
Tirunesh Dibaba	(1985–)
Long-distance runner and Olympic gold medalist	
Haile Gebrselassie	(1973–)
Marathon runner and Olympic gold medalist	
Haile Selassie	(1892–1975)
Emperor	
Birtukan Mideksa	(1974–)
Lawyer and political activist	
Afewerk Tekle	(1932–2012)
Artist	

Clockwise from top: **Currency, Tirunesh Dibaba, schoolchildren**

To Find Out More

Books

▶ Laird, Elizabeth. *When the World Began: Stories Collected in Ethiopia*. New York: Oxford University Press, 2000.

▶ Thimmesh, Catherine. *Lucy Long Ago: Uncovering the Mystery of Where We Came From*. New York: Houghton Mifflin Harcourt, 2009.

Music

▶ Astatke, Mulatu. *Sketches of Ethiopia*. Paris: Jazz Village, 2013.

▶ Aweke, Aster. *Ewedihalehu*. Portland, OR: CD Baby, 2013.

▶ *The Rough Guide to the Music of Ethiopia*. London: World Music Network, 2012.

▶ Visit this Scholastic website for more information on Ethiopia:
www.factsfornow.scholastic.com
Enter the keyword **Ethiopia**

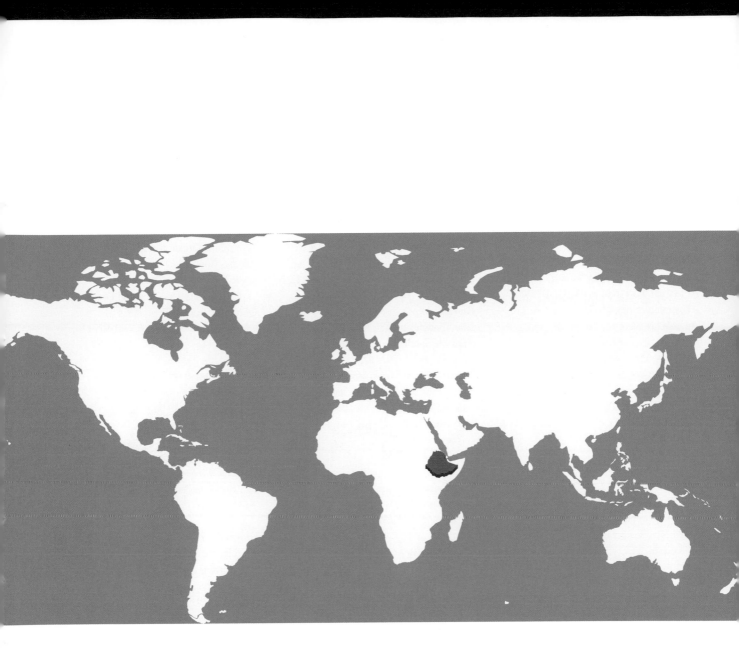

Index

Page numbers in *italics* indicate illustrations.

hummingbirds, 28
hyenas, 101
Lake Tana, 21
livestock, *17*, 71–72
mountain nyala, 38, *38*
mountains, 37, 38, *38, 39*
pelicans, *32*
rock art, 103
rodents, 35
Simien foxes, 37, 39, *39*
vultures, 32–33
walia ibex, 37, *37*
warthogs, 34
wattled ibis, 33
antelopes, 34
archaeology, 42, *42*, 104
architecture, 107, 108
Ark of the Covenant, 97, *97*, 99, 126
Armah (king), 100
art, 103–105, *105*, 106–109, *107, 108, 109*, 133
artisanal manufacturing, 73–74
Arum lily. *See* calla lily.
Aster Aweke, 113, *113*
Awash National Park, 18, 25
Awash River, 16, 25, 77
Awash Valley, 41, 42
azmaris (musicians), 110

B

Bahir Dar, 119
Bale Mountains, *14*, 28, 37, 38, 39
Bale Mountains National Park, 25
banded barbets, 33
Baro River, 19
baskets, 68, 79, 109
Battle of Adwa, 48, 49, *49*, 50
beads, *116*, 122
bees, 72
begena (musical instrument), 110, 111
belg season, 23
berbere (spice mixture), 120
Berhale, 76

birds, 28, 32–33, *32*
Birtukan Mideksa, 57, *57*, 133
blackwinged lovebirds, 33
bleeding heart monkey. *See* gelada.
Blue Nile Falls. *See* Tissisat Falls.
Blue Nile River, 19, 20–21, 77, *77*, 78
blue-winged geese, 33
body paint, 9
borders, 11
buzzards, 32–33

C

calendar, 125
calla lily (national flower), 28, *28*
camels, *17*, 76, *76*, 90
capital city. *See* Addis Ababa.
cattle, 71, 88, 103, 122
cell phones, 83, *83*
children, *6*, 87, *87*, 118, 119, *123*
Christianity
    Aksum Kingdom and, 44
    Ark of the Covenant, 97, *97*, 99, 126
    arrival of, 44
    art and, 103–105, *105*, 107
    Church of St. George, 98
    conversion to, 94
    Coptics, 104
    Daga Estefanos monastery, 99
    Debre Damo monastery, 45, *45*
    Easter, *92*
    Ethiopian Orthodox Church, 9, 44–45, 92, 93, *94*, 95, 96, 97, *97*, 99, 103, *111*, 113
    Ezana (emperor) and, 94–95
    Frumentius and, 95, *95*
    Guardian of the Ark, 97
    holidays, 126
    holy spring, 20
    Holy Trinity Cathedral, 62
    Islam and, 8–9, 100–101, 105
    Iyasu and, 50
    jihad and, 46
    language and, 113

literature and, 114
Menelik I and, 97
missionaries, 47, *47*, 94, 95, 105, 114
monasteries, 45, *45*, 99
music and, 110, *111*
population, 93
Portugal and, 46
Protestantism, 93
Roman Catholic Church, 46, 93
Ten Commandments, 97
Timket festival, 96, 126–127, *127*
Ura Kidane Meret (church), 99
Zadok (priest), 97
Church of St. George, 98
cities. *See also* Addis Ababa; villages.
    Aksum, 68, 94, 95, 97
    Bahir Dar, 119
    Dire Dawa, 67, 119
    Gondar, 18, *18*, 40, 86, *109*
    Harar, 101, *101*, 107, 109, 122
    Hawassa, 86, 119
    Jimma, 119
    Lalibela, 44, *91*, 98, *98*
    Massawa, 48
    Mekele, 18, *18, 72*, 86, 119
    Nazret, 18, 86
civil war, 55, 59
climate, 12, 22–25, 27, 54, 72, 86
climate change, 30, 72
clothing, *100*, 108, 122
Coalition for Unity and Democracy, 57
coffee
    ceremony, 120, *120*
    industry, 30, 50, 52–53, 70–71, 73, 74, 79, *80, 81*
    plant, 29, 30, *30*
College of Performing and Visual Arts, 106
communications, 52, 83, *83*, 114
communism, 53, 59
constitution, 54, 55, 59
construction industry, 69
Coptic Christians, 104
Council of Ministers, 65

religious, 126–127
Holy Trinity Cathedral, 62
Homo sapiens, 41
honey, 72, *72*, 120
Horn of Africa, 11
House of Federation, 63
House of Peoples' Representatives, 63, 64
housing, 86, *104*
hummingbirds, 28
hydroelectricity, *19*, 21, 77–78, *77*
hydrothermal fields, 16
hyenas, 101

I

"An Imagined Story" (Afawark Gabra
   Iyasus), 115
immunizations, 87
imports, 18, 80
independence, 85
infrastructure, 82–83
injera (flatbread), 119–120, *119*
insect life, 34
internet, 83
irrigation, 17, 21, 43
Islam
   Ahmed Gragn, 46
   Aksumite Empire and, 100
   Aksum Kingdom and, 44
   arrival of, 44
   calendar, 126
   Christianity and, 8–9, 100–101, 105
   clothing and, *100*, 122
   Eastern Lowlands, 101
   Eid al-Fitr, 126
   Harar, 101, 109
   holidays, 126
   Iyasu and, 50
   jihad, 46
   mosques, 101, *101*
   Muhammad (prophet), 100
   population, 93, 101
   Portugal and, 46

Qur'an (holy book), *100*
Ramadan, 126
Sharia courts, 66–67
Tewodros II and, 47
Italian Somaliland, 51
Italy, 48–49, 50–51
Iyasu (emperor), 50

J

jerricans, *118*
Jimma, 119
Judaism, 93–94, 96
judicial branch of government, 59, 65, 67

K

Karo people, 9, *110*, 122
Kebede Mikael, 115
kebero (musical instrument), *102*, 110
Kebra Negast (national epic), 94
Kenticha mine, 75
khat plant, 71, 79
Kobar Sink, 12
kremt season, 23

L

Lake Abaya, 22
Lake Abe, 22
Lake Awash, 22
Lake Shala, 12
Lake Tana, 12, 19, 20, 21, *21*, 35, 99
Lake Ziway, 18
Lalibela (city), 44, *91*, 98, *98*, *108*
Lalibela (king), 44, 72
languages, *20*, 42, 48, 62, 67, 90, 91, *91*,
   95, 113, 114
League of Nations, 50
legislative branch of government, 59, 63,
   67
Libb-waled tarik (An Imagined Story)
   (Afawark Gabra Iyasus), 115
lion baboon. *See* gelada.
Lion of Judah statue, *58*

lip plates, 88, *88*
literacy rate, 118
literature, 94, 114, 115
livestock, *17*, 28, 71–72, *71*, 88
local governments, 67
Lucy (hominid), 42, *42*
Lulu, Solomon, 60

M

Mahmoud Ahmed, 112
Makonnen Endalkachew, 115
manufacturing, 18, 73–74, *73*
maps. *See also* historical maps.
   Addis Ababa, *62*
   geopolitical, *8*
   population density, *86*
   resources, *75*
   topographical, *12*
"March Forward, Dear Mother Ethiopia"
   (national anthem), 60
marine life, 21, *32*
masenqo (musical instrument), 110
Massawa, 48
Mekele, 18, *18*, *72*, 86, 119
Meles Zenawi, 55
Menelik I (emperor), 41–42, 44, 93–94, 97
Menelik II (emperor), 48–49, *49*, 51, 62
Mengistu Gedamu, 115
Mengistu Haile Mariam, 53, 54
metric system, 81
microbial life, 16
military, 53, 65, 113
mining, 74–75, 76, *76*, 77
Ministry of Health, 87
missionaries, 47, *47*, 94, 95, 105, 114
Mitsawa. *See* Massawa.
monasteries, 45, *45*, 99
monkeys, 33, 34
mosques, 101, *101*
mountain nyala, 38, *38*
Mount Batu, 17
Mount Ras Dejen, 16

Meet the Author

Lura Rogers Seavey has been fascinated with Africa ever since her parents traveled there when she was a young child. Her parents brought home traditional handwoven baskets, handmade spears, carvings, masks, and even a three-foot-tall wooden tool used to grind flour by hand.

Seavey studied at Skidmore College and Harvard University where she earned a bachelor of arts degree, and has begun graduate work in sustainability and environmental science. She has written several books in the Enchantment of the World series, including *Czech Republic*, *Nigeria*, *Switzerland*, *Spain*, and *Dominican Republic*. She is also the author of *More Than Petticoats: Remarkable Massachusetts Women*, a collection of short biographies.

Seavey is a coffee lover who seeks out Ethiopian Yirgacheffe whenever possible.

Photo Credits

Photographs ©: cover: hadynyah/iStockphoto; back cover: urosr/iStockphoto; 2: Jon Bratt/Moment Open/Getty Images; 4 left: Mike Korostelev www.mkorostelev.com/Moment/Getty Images; 4 center: Eric Lafforgue/Alamy Images; 4 right: ooyoo/E+/Getty Images; 5 left: Grant Rooney Premium/Alamy Images; 5 right: Nigel Pavitt/AWL Images/Getty Images; 6: hadynyah/iStockphoto; 9: Sylvain Cordier/The Image Bank/Getty Images; 10: Nigel Pavitt/AWL Images; 13: Philippe Bourseiller/The Image Bank/Getty Images; 14: Nigel Pavitt/AWL Images/Getty Images; 15: Mike Korostelev www.mkorostelev.com/Moment/Getty Images; 16: Loic Poidevin/Minden Pictures; 17: itpow/iStockphoto; 18 top: Ariadne Van Zandbergen/Lonely Planet Images/Getty Images; 18 bottom: Frank Metois/Alamy Images; 19: Nigel Pavitt/AWL Images/Getty Images; 20: Sybil Sassoon/robertharding/age fotostock; 21: Nigel Pavitt/AWL Images; 22: Eric Lafforgue/Art in All of Us/Corbis News/Getty Images; 23: Frances Linzee Gordon/Lonely Planet Images/Getty Images; 24: Dereje Belachew/Alamy Images; 25: Nigel Pavitt/AWL Images/Getty Images; 26: Nigel Pavitt/AWL Images/Getty Images; 28: ooyoo/E+/Getty Images; 29: Nigel Pavitt/AWL Images; 30: Eric Lafforgue/Gamma-Rapho/Getty Images; 31: Danita Delimont/Alamy Images; 32: Joel Carillet/iStockphoto; 33: Ajlber/Fotosearch LBRF/age fotostock; 34: Juergen Ritterbach/Alamy Images; 35: Christ Grodotzki/dpa picture alliance/Alamy Images; 36: Thomas Marent/Minden Pictures; 37: guenterguni/Vetta/Getty Images; 38: Gabrielle Therin-Weise/Photographer's Choice RF/Getty Images; 39 top: Will Burrard-Lucas/Minden Pictures; 39 bottom: Laurent Geslin/Minden Pictures; 40: MJ Photography/Alamy Images; 42: Ariadne Van Zandbergen/Lonely Planet Images/Getty Images; 43: Martin Harvey/Gallo Images/Getty Images; 45: Patrick Robert - Corbis/Sygma/Getty Images; 47: Corbis Historical/Getty Images; 49: The Art Archive/Superstock, Inc.; 51: Bettmann/Getty Images; 52: Michael Ochs Archives/Getty Images; 54: Keystone Pictures/Alamy Images; 55: Les Stone/The Image Works; 56: Elias Meseret/dpa/age fotostock; 57: Samson Haileyesus/AP Images; 58: Andy Chadwick/Alamy Images; 60: Simon Maina/AFP/Getty Images; 61: Zacharias Abubeker/AFP/Getty Images; 62 top: FrankvandenBergh/E+/Getty Images; 63: Zacharias Abubeker/AFP/Getty Images; 64: Zacharias Abubeker/AFP/Getty Images; 65: Poligrafistka/DigitalVision Vectors/Getty Images; 66: Photoshot/TopFoto/The Image Works; 68: Bruno Barbier/robertharding/Getty Images; 70: Bilal Hussein/AP Images; 71: Ton Koene/age fotostock/Superstock, Inc.; 72: Zacharias Abubeker/AFP/Getty Images; 73: Kay Nietfeld/dpa/Alamy Images; 76 bottom: Ignacio Marin/Anadolu Agency/Getty Images; 76 top: Eric Baccega/Minden Pictures; 77: Gioia Forster/dpa/Alamy Images; 78: Constantinos Petrinos/Minden Pictures; 79: Ivan Vdovin/Alamy Images; 80: Edwin Remsberg/age fotostock; 81: Richard Human/Alamy Images; 82: Minasse Wondimu Hailu/Anadolu Agency/Getty Images; 83: Buena Vista Images/The Image Bank/Getty Images; 84: Minasse Wondimu Hailu/Anadolu Agency/Getty Images; 87: Mike Goldwater/Alamy Images; 88: Carl De Souza/AFP/Getty Images; 89: Nigel Pavitt/AWL Images/Getty Images; 91: hadynyah/E+/Getty Images; 92: Panayiotis Tzamaros/Pacific Press/Light Rocket/Getty Images; 94: Novarc Images/Alamy Images; 95: Paul Fearn/Alamy Images; 96: Carl De Souza/AFP/Getty Images; 97 top: Toby Adamson/Axiom Photographic/age fotostock; 97 bottom: PhotoStock-Israel/Alamy Images; 98: imageBROKER/Alamy Images; 99: Amar Grover/AWL Images/Getty Images; 100: Grant Rooney Premium/Alamy Images; 101: Anthony Pappone/Moment/Getty Images; 102: Nigel Pavitt/AWL Images; 104: Eric Lafforgue/Alamy Images; 105: robertharding/Superstock, Inc.; 107: age fotostock/Alamy Images; 108: Eitan Simanor/Alamy Images; 109: Patrick Syder/Lonely Planet Images/Getty Images; 110: John Warburton-Lee/AWL Images/Getty Images; 111: Dereje Belachew/Alamy Images; 112: PYMCA/UIG/Getty Images; 113: Jack Vartoogian/Getty Images; 114: G Walts/Syracuse Newspapers/The Image Works; 116: Ben Pipe Photography/Cultura Exclusive/Getty Images; 118: Melanie Stetson Freeman/The Christian Science Monitor/Getty Images; 119: John Elk/Lonely Planet Images/Getty Images; 120: Photononstop/Alamy Images; 121: LOOK Die Bildagentur der Fotografen GmbH/Alamy Images; 123: David Sacks/The Image Bank/Getty Images; 124: Simon Balson/Alamy Images; 125: Peter Delarue/AFP/Getty Images; 127: Jon Bratt/Moment Open/Getty Images; 130 left: Poligrafistka/DigitalVision Vectors/Getty Images; 130 right: Zacharias Abubeker/AFP/Getty Images; 131 right: Nigel Pavitt/AWL Images; 133 top left: Ivan Vdovin/Alamy Images; 133 right: Simon Balson/Alamy Images; 133 bottom left: hadynyah/E+/Getty Images.

Maps by Mapping Specialists.